The Collector's Encyclopedia of

SALT & PEPPER

SHAKERS

FIGURAL AND NOVELTY

Melva Davern

COLLECTOR BOOKS

A Division of Schroeder Publishing Co., Inc.

The current values in this book should be used only as a guide. They are not intended to set prices, which vary from one section of the country to another. Auction prices as well as dealer prices vary greatly and are affected by condition as well as demand. Neither the Author nor the Publisher assumes responsibility for any losses that might be incurred as a result of consulting this guide.

Additional copies of this book may be ordered from:

Collector Books
P.O. Box 3009
Paducah, KY 42002-3009
or
Melva Davern
Box 81914
Pittsburgh, PA 15217

@ $19.95. Add $2.00 for postage and handling.

Copyright: Melva R. Davern, 1985
Values Updated, 1991

Acknowledgments

Since there were *so* many people along the way who have helped, this is a very difficult part of this book to write. I guess it's best just to start at the beginning and thank everyone in the order that they became involved as the book progressed. But first of all, I want to thank Bill Schroeder for giving me the opportunity to fulfill a life-long dream of having my work published.

Many thanks to my family for allowing me to share them with you throughout this book: my husband George, my children Laura, George, Jr., Jack and Jason. To my parents John and Barbara Beynon for their constant encouragement and many wonderful memories. To my sister and brothers, Joanne Thiry, Jack and Bill Beynon; and a special note of thanks to my sister Dee Himelright who has helped me in too many ways to mention. Love and kisses to the dearest little old lady in the world, Katherine Evans, my ninety-three-year-old Grandmother, who has been an inspiration to five generations of our family.

Although all my children have "lived" salt and pepper shakers, I must give my twelve-year-old son, Jack, a very special "thankyou." When you take a child into an antique shop or show, heads usually turn to see if he will break something or misbehave. Jack has gone everywhere with me since he was eight years old and he has won the love and respect of many dealers with his wit and infectious smile. He has become an asset to me beyond what words can express, and I thank him and hope he never grows out of being himself.

Thanks to all the people that sold me their collections throughout the years, and to all those who helped me pack, unpack and sort. Special thanks to my friend Pat Shilling who helped me pack up a collection of 4,000 shakers. It took two trips to get them all home where we then unpacked them. (Buying collections HAS been an adventure!)

I have friends who have helped me with pricing, identification and, most of all, encouragement: Jacquie Greenwood, Muriel White, Fred Roerig, Marcia Smith, Jeannie Fouts, Theresa Knox, Elaine Godwin and Larry Carey.

To my friends in Pittsburgh who generously offered so much support: Sandy and Dale Lovas and all my friends from Tam's. The mail carriers from the Pittsburgh Squirrel Hill Station not only encouraged me, they also led me to some great house sales in the area! To my neighbors and the many flea market and antique dealers who were always ready to help in any way, my thanks to all of you.

In order to have the best photography available for this book, I took the shakers to Kentucky to be professionally done. Since my husband could not make the trip with me, my best friend (for twenty-seven years!) offered to go. So many thanks to Rose Hertzer for her help in reading the map and getting us to Paducah in spite of all bets against our making it. She was a real asset to me in many ways: packing, unpacking, keeping notes and most of all helping to make a very long trip enjoyable and memorable . . .

Tom Clouser of Curtis & Mays Studio in Paducah was responsible for the great photographs throughout the book. I thank him for his patience and his wonderful sense of humor and I forgive him for that bit about the "salt and pepper thieves."

Also, many thanks to Jane White and Steve Quertermous from Schroeder Publishing. Their combined efforts in arranging the material, designing the cover and their great sense of organization in an area hitherto unfamiliar to me helped make this book possible.

Writing this book has been an experience, to say the least. Most writers have a knack for composing stories or poetry or whatever. Even creators of some of the greatest literary works of art, however, may suffer from certain deficiencies. Even though they may not admit it, a number of writers have dreadful handwriting, cannot type and may even be unable to spell. I will be honest enough to admit it that I suffer from all three . . . and therefore, my overwhelming appreciation goes to the last person involved in writing this book. My very dear and loyal friend Mary Schinhofen, has edited, corrected spelling, reworded and, finally typed this entire book. Anyone who has ever received one of my personal letters (unedited) will attest to the fact that this was no easy task! I have no doubt that without her help this book would have gone to print at a much later date. For everything, Mary, I thank you.

To all of you, I hope you find this book worthy of your help and encouragement throughout the years but, most of all, I hope that you find that it was indeed worth waiting for . . .

Introduction

Welcome to the world of figural and novelty salt and pepper shakers! My primary purpose in writing this book is to provide some source of reference for the veteran collector who has been neglected too long. Although most of the figural and novelty salt and pepper sets were made from about the 1920's through the 1960's--not such a long time ago--we have literally had to go on a seek-and-search mission to secure any information on our collections. Yearly price guides give a little information, but nothing really concrete nor especially enlightening. Little has been done based strictly on novelty/figural sets. It is my hope that this book will help fulfill this need.

Secondly, this book is for the specialized collector, for the novice collector just starting out and even for people looking for something to collect. Salt and peppers offer such a wide range of possibilities that there is truly something for everyone. You may choose to collect only sets of bisque, wood, metal or bone china. Maybe a specialized area such as Occupied Japan, miniature beer bottles, Black Americana or nodders apppeals to you. Whatever it may happen to be, the choice is yours to make.

In addition, I hope this book will inspire some respect for these fanciful objects. I want to see more people hold on to "Mom's old collection." Everytime I buy a collection from someone, I try to get all the information I can about it. To whom did it belong? How long did they collect salt and peppers? Why are they selling the collection? I have bought collections from some of the most lovable people in the world. Sometimes I get so involved, I end up in tears before I get out of the house. But, at least they know when I leave, I will treasure their collection as much as they did. One thing I always do before I pack up a collection is to ask if there is any set that has special sentimental value. If so, I insist they keep it--there may not be room for an entire collection, but there is always room for a memory!

People have begun collecting salt and peppers for many reasons. Some collections are inherited and then continued. Some people make the decision for you--they see two or three sets around your home and tell everyone you collect salt and peppers and suddenly you do. Regardless of how you get started, they are interesting to collect. In some areas of salt and pepper collecting, your initial investment can also prove to be quite profitable in the future.

More than anything, I hope you enjoy my book. I will welcome any of your letters. Hearing about other collections prompted this book. I have accumulated information from many sources over the past few years. As accurate as we may try to be, we are not always right. In the same vein I am sure there are things I should have included, but didn't. So, all of your comments and correspondence are welcome--good or bad.

Prices listed are just a guide of current market values, compiled and averaged from many areas of the country. It is not necessarily what you should pay or charge for any particular set. The availability of certain sets may be better in some areas, causing a difference in the price range. Trends in collecting also cause price fluctuations, as in the case of Occupied Japan and black memorabilia.

Hints for the Collector

Do not remove manufacturer or import company tags, labels or stickers. The information printed on them will be helpful to future collectors. Price tags, unless printed by the manufacturer or distributor, do not necessarily fall into this category--although it's always nice to know how much a set of shakers originally cost in the retail stores.

Be extremely careful in cleaning old shakers. Never soak shakers in water--soaking can often remove the paint. If you are certain that the paint is under-glaze rather than over-glaze, use a very soft toothbrush to clean the grooves in detailed pieces. Unless the shakers are very dirty, however, it is best just to use a damp cloth to wipe them clean. Do not use detergents. Be very careful with metal, wood and chalkware sets; water should never, ever be used on these materials.

As soon as you buy them, always empty all condiments and pieces from the shakers. Salt, for example, is extremely corrosive and can destroy many shakers if stored for a long time.

In any set, the salt shaker always has either more holes and/or larger holes and is usually the larger shaker in the pair. Salt is coarse, therefore requiring a larger opening, and is used in greater quantities than pepper. Pepper, on the other hand, is very finely ground and is used more sparingly. Always try to make sure that it IS a pair of shakers that you are buying. If the holes are identical, you are most likely buying two salts or two peppers.

Although the import companies were not listed for each set pictured in this book, most of the shakers were made in Japan. In a future publication, a list of the many different import companies will be included. Because many different companies may have sold the same type sets, I felt it was not an asset to list the import company or distributor with each shaker--especially since this type of identification can be extremely confusing to the beginning collector.

Keep records on your collection; when and where you bought each set, how much you paid, any distinguishing characteristics or variations and any markings found on it. When buying collections, try to get all the information you can to help in dating the sets. Often no one knows more about the shakers you are purchasing than the person who originally owned them. As your experience grows, you will be better able to separate fact from fiction--but, in the meantime, learn all you can from the seller.

When buying new shakers which are issued in a "series," try to locate and purchase all the sets; if this is not possible, keep an accurate list of those you know to be available. This type of information which will be invaluable to collectors of the future. With the passing of time, our "new" collections will become "old" collections, and, without some effort on our part now, too much information will be lost. A complete list of the "series shakers" produced twenty or thirty years ago would help us, but unfortunately, the original manufacturers are either out of business or have kept very incomplete records. As collectors, we have the inclination to collect the objects, but we also have the duty to collect the information for future generations.

Don't hesitate in buying shakers that are offered for a limited time only--such as advertising sets or premiums. Buy them as soon as they are offered. You won't get a second chance on the primary market!

Remember--there are probably very few households in the United States without at least ONE set of salt and pepper shakers and some have thousands . . . I know! Happy collecting!

Table of Contents

Section One

Section Two - People

Advertising

The mini Sealtest bottles remind me of a plant that was not more than five minutes from where I lived. It, like many of the small dairies and bottling plants, closed several years ago when home delivery service was stopped. The memories of my old neighborhood make this set doubly precious.

The plastic Heinz Ketchup bottles were not authorized by the H.J. Heinz Company and, normally, I would not show an unauthorized item. This, however is a product that is so much a part of my home town that I just HAD to include them. Running out of Heinz ketchup in my house creates a major crisis that only a quick trip to the supermarket will remedy. This set was made in Hong Kong for the retail market in the late 1970's.

Another one of my favorites is the Hershey Kisses, sold in Hershey, Pennsylvania as a souvenir from the chocolate factory. The ceramic replicas are not as good to eat--but they are rather unique.

"A bee and a bye and a bo and a bop and a Dairy Queen with a curl on top." Remember that jingle? And you have your choice of vanilla (salt) or chocolate (pepper). The third set on the second shelf is "Chicken of the Sea" tuna. The words are imprinted on the bottom of the set and appear to be from the 1940's.

The blue gas flames pictured in the center of the page were a 1940's promotion for a gas company. I have also seen this in a sugar, creamer and a spoon rest; "Handy Flame" is impressed on most of the items.

The G.E. coil top refrigerator, produced in the late 1920's, is made of milk glass. A set with the original G.E. logo sticker on the front increases the value.

The Greyhound Buses on the next shelf are all metal with movable wheels. Since the paint is very worn on most of the sets I have seen, it appears that this is a difficult set to find in mint condition but keep trying!

Since advertising is a part of our lives and is seemingly everywhere, these sets are familiar to most of us. If you plan to collect in this area, however, remember that promotional sets are offered for just a short time in most cases--so don't hesitate in buying them as soon as they appear! Most of the sets here were also sold in retail stores as souvenir items and date from the early 1930's to the present.

Row 1: (1) Sealtest minis, $15.00-18.00   (2) Heinz Ketchup, $8.00-10.00   (3)Ball Mason minis, $25.00-28.00

Row 2: (2) Dairy Queen, $8.00-10.00   (2) Hershey Kisses, $6.00-8.00   (3) Chicken of the Sea, $15.00-18.00

Row 3: (1) General Electric, $35.00-40.00   (2) Handy Flame, $20.00-22.00   (3) Toaster, $12.00-15.00

Row 4: (1) Greyhound buses, $40.00-45.00   (2) Westinghouse washer/dryer, $12.00-15.00   (3) Firestone tires, $12.00-15.00

Row 5: (1) Pepsi bottles (full), $3.00-5.00   (2) 7-up bottles, $3.00-5.00   (3) Pepsi bottles (clear), $3.00-5.00

Advertising: F & F Plastics

The Fiedler and Fiedler Mold and Die Works of Dayton, Ohio, produces many advertising items for companies to use as premiums or giveaways. All the items pictured on this page are from F & F and their logo is imprinted on the bottom of each piece.

All of the F & F sets are plastic and were all made in the U.S.A. The design and decoration are very well done. However, since the paint is applied over a solid color base, it is not unusual to find paint wear on most of the sets. The items pictured here are what I consider to be the ONLY "official" Aunt Jemima and Uncle Mose items and the F & F logo is on the bottom of every item. Other kitchen items such as recipe boxes, notepad holders, etc., found by collectors were manufactured elsewhere. I have included in this section, however, all of the Aunt Jemima and Uncle Mose collectibles known to have been produced by the F & F Co.

This line was produced in the 1950's to promote Aunt Jemima Pancake Mix. The pieces were made available to the public as a premium for sending in boxtops. The Quaker Oats Company, however, also sponsored breakfast parties to promote the pancake mix and additional items could be purchased at the parties.

The spice set on its original rack and the cookie jar are blue chip pieces to collectors. The large and small salt and peppers are still fairly easy to find, but prices are rising fast. The syrup pitcher, the first item produced in the line, was taped to the top of every box of Aunt Jemima Pancake Mix. The entire set of the two-piece sugar and creamer is difficult to find. Quite often I have found sets with missing lids. Finding the complete F & F kitchen set is very rare. Even though some of the pieces are unrelated to salt and peppers, I have featured this set because it is so unusual to find everything in the entire line pictured together.

The premiums were discontinued in the early 1960's. With the growth of the Civil Rights Movement, items such as this were considered racially objectionable. The Quaker Oats Company, therefore, stopped the production of the entire line. Aunt Jemima has been a part of our lives for a very long time. (Her name was taken from a dance tune titled "Aunt Jemima.") Her history began in the late 1880's and continues even today as collectors gather together as many Aunt Jemima artifacts as possible. She may be a stereotype but she made some of the best pancakes I ever tasted!

On the bottom row is a set of "Luzianne Mammy." Produced in the early 1950's, this set was a promotional item for the now-defunct Luzianne Coffee Company. The shakers pictured are original; BEWARE of reproductions, which have red skirts instead of the green skirts shown. In addition, the words "Luzianne Mammy" are impressed on the originals--and ONLY on the originals. Collectors of Black Americana consider this to be a hard-to-find set and, as such, it commands a high price.

On the same shelf we find Willie and Millie Penguin produced in the early 1940's to promote Kool cigarettes. Fido and Fifi, available in the 1950's, were manufactured to advertise Ken-L Ration Pet Food Company. Although these shakers are very nostalgically appealing, the next set--the Campbell Kids--are one of my favorites. Like "Aunt Jemima," the Campbell Kids have been a part of our lives for a very long time. Originating in 1905, they have delighted eight generations of children, but have never aged themselves! Their bright little well-fed faces are recognized all over the world.

This set of Campbell Kid shakers is one any collector would cherish. In addition, however, there is a complete line of Campbell Kids items on the market and several collector clubs also exist. Hopefully the Kids will remain a symbol of Campbell Soups for years to come, so that our grandchildren and the generations to follow will be able to love them as we have.

Row 1: (1) $50.00-65.00 each   (2) Cookie jar $300.00-350.00   (3) $50.00-65.00 each

Row 2: (1) Spice Set as pictured $400.00-450.00   (2) Single shakers $40.00-45.00 each

Row 3: (1) $45.00-50.00   (2) $45.00-50.00 (syrup)   (3) $35.00-40.00 each

Row 4: (1) $100.00-125.00   (2) $10.00-12.00   (3) $10.00-12.00   (4) 35.00-40.00

Advertising: Figural Sets

Collecting advertising salt-and-pepper sets can be rewarding in many ways. First of all, that old nostalgia always pops up when you look at some of the famous characters that represent products we have used throughout the years. Think about the advertising personalities that have worked their way into our hearts: Aunt Jemima, Nipper, Mr. Peanut, the Campbell Kids, Elsie the Borden Cow and so many others. Many of them have been around longer than we have. Secondly, collecting these little prizes is just plain fun and, of course, they have proved to be very sound investments. The prices for these sets just keep going up, up and up!

Beginning with one of the most famous and beloved advertising symbols of all time, let's take a look at Nipper. Nipper has been around since the early 1900's and in 1929, he became the trademark for RCA after their purchase of the Victor Talking Machine Company. He now appears on all RCA products. The first set shown in Row Four was put out by the Lenox China Company. The other set is ceramic and is marked "Radio Corporation of America." It dates from the 1940's.

The Borden Company gave us the lovable Elsie in 1937. Her husband Elmer and baby Beauregard were added in the 1940's. The sets pictured are copyright 1940, The Borden Company. Sadly, except for Elsie, the rest of the family gradually disappeared and the only sign left of Elmer is carried on Borden's well-known glue. Both of these sets, however, are a delightful find for collectors of advertising.

The set of plastic salt and peppers depicting Colonel Harland Sanders was copyrighted in 1965 by Kentucky Fried Chicken. (I have also found a set dated 1971 which has a red bottom on the pepper shaker.) The Colonel traveled all over the United States selling his famous chicken recipe to restaurants. After a rather humble beginning in the 1930's and after 30 years of selling his recipe, Sanders became the trademark of the Kentuckey Fried Chicken chain that began in the 1960's. Since then, it has become one of the largest fast food chains in the world.

Poppin' and Poppie Fresh are new compared to the others. Poppin' Fresh was originally known as the "Pillsbury Doughboy" in the1960's. In 1972 his name was changed to Poppin' and Poppie Fresh was added to the family. The sets shown are copyrighted 1974, The Pillsbury Company. The ceramic set was sold in retail stores but the plastic sets were given as premiums for labels.

Bert and Harry, in the center of the third row, were issued in 1970 by Peils Beer. This set is a real treasure for collectors. It is recent, but I don't believe many of them were made. This set traveled from the White House to be included in this book--the Muriel and Rich White house, that is. Most of the sets on this page were borrowed from the Whites' collection of advertising sets.

The other sets more or less speak for themselves. The "Sunshine Bakers," third set in the second row, have their names written across the fronts of their hats, but it doesn't show up well on the photograph. This set and "Bert and Harry" were made in Japan. Colonel Sanders was made in Canada. Most of the other sets are American-made. I found that before 1960 most American companies had all their advertising premiums and promotions manufactured in this country.

Row 1: (1) $35.00-40.00 set	(2) $45.00-50.00	(3) $35.00-40.00 set
Row 2: (1) $35.00-40.00	(2) $65.00-70.00	(3) $15.00-18.00
Row 3: (1) $18.00-20.00	(2) $40.00-45.00	(3) $15.00-18.00
Row 4: (1) $45.00-50.00	(2) $18.00-20.00	(3) $45.00-50.00

Advertising: Mini Beers

At least one or two sets of mini beers find their way into every general collection of salt and peppers. If they seem to be an odd brand, it's a good idea to check them out--they may be more valuable than you think! The most sought after bottles are those with the metal caps; the bottles with plastic caps are reproductions made in Taiwan in the 70's.

The market for minature beer sets was supplied mainly by two companies: Edward A. Muth & Sons, Inc. of Buffalo, New York, and Bill's Novelty & Premium Company of Milwaukee, Wisconsin. The company name is usually embossed on the bottom of the bottles, along with code numbers which help date them. The Muth minis, which were made from 1933 to 1963, all had metal S & P caps. Breweries bought the sets and used them as giveaways and/or premiums.

Bill's bottles, on the other hand, mostly had solid caps. Many contained a liquid to represent beer. At first, they were sold to breweries to be used a premiums but were later sold to variety stores as novelties and souvenirs. Bill's distributed the bottles from about 1939 to 1956. The labels on the mini beers include breweries from at least 33 states, the District of Columbia, and several foreign countries. All bottles from both companies are made in the United States.

The value of the minis varies according to age, the label, condition, manufacturer and availability. People who collect breweriana usually require one bottle of each type for their collection; S & P collectors, however, want both shakers.

Considering the wealth of information available concerning these shakers, I cound not begin to scratch the surface in this book. If you intend to collect minis seriously, I must recommend a book devoted to this subject. Titled *Miniature Beer Bottles and Go-withs*, this book includes research on breweries, manufacturers, dates and exhaustive background. Written by Robert E. Kay and privately printed, this publication is the most informative and well-written one available on this subject, and it includes a price guide. I would also like to extend my personal thanks to Mr. Kay for updating the values for the bottles in this book and for his invaluable background information.

You will notice that there is quite a variety to choose from in this section. The E & O, Gold Bond and 4¼" Falstaff are among those minis which are hard to find and therefore merit a very high price. The 4" Schlitz and 3" Fort Pitt, on the other hand, are much more common.

There is a lot of competition connected with collecting these little beer bottles. Collectors of advertising, miniatures, breweriana, bottles and plain old nostalgia, as well as the salt and pepper collectors, are all searching for them, making them increasingly difficult to find. That is one of the things, of course, that makes collecting so much fun . . . the challenge of finding it first!

Row 1: (1) $50.00-75.00	(2) $12.00-16.00	(3) $16.00-20.00	(4) $8.00-12.00	(5) $8.00-12.00
Row 2: (1) $5.00-8.00	(2) $3.00-5.00	(3) $3.00-5.00	(4) $3.00-5.00	(5) $8.00-12.00
Row 3: (1) $8.00-12.00	(2) $8.00-12.00	(3) $8.00-12.00	(4) $8.00-12.00	(5) $20.00-30.00
Row 4: (1) $8.00-12.00	(2) $12.00-16.00	(3) $12.00-16.00	(4) $8.00-12.00	(5) $50.00-75.00
Row 5: (1) $8.00-12.00	(2) $5.00-8.00	(3) $12.00-16.00	(4) $12.00-16.00	(5) $8.00-12.00

Advertising: Pumps and Peanuts

Miniature gas pumps are fast becoming one of the favorites in the advertising world. With the closing of so many small oil companies in the last several years and the merging of many others, these sets are a reminder of all the obsolete companies of the past. They are often found with the name of a service station imprinted on the back. Originally given to customers as gifts or premiums with the sale of gas, these sets eventually were sold in retail stores as souvenir or novelty items.

Using a magnifying glass, I could just make out the numbers on the Phillips 66 sets. It reads "13 gallons--$3.54." With a little quick figuring, I discovered that totaled about 27 cents per gallon. REMEMBER WHEN!

Notice the set of Pyroflex pumps--the only one I have ever seen of this type. All of the sets, popular in the 1940's and 1950's, are plastic and made in the U.S.A.

The sets on the last three shelves are all Mr. Peanut in various forms. Mr. Peanut is the symbol for the Planters Peanut Company which opened in 1906 in Wilkes-Barre, Pennsylvania. The owners, Amedeo Obici and Mario Peruzzi, set out to find a trademark to help promote and identify their product. A local schoolboy made a sketch of a peanut character; it was then given to a commercial artist who added the monocle and crossed leg. In 1916 "Mr. Peanut" made his first appearance. Since then, every product distributed by the Planters Peanut Company carries this symbol. He has without a doubt earned the honor of being called "Mister."

There are thousands of Mr. Peanut collectibles and several clubs have been formed by collectors of this wonderful character. Premiums are constantly being offered by the Planters Company in exchange for wrappers, etc. A book titled *Planters Peanuts Advertising and Collectibles* was printed in 1978 and would be a definite asset to anyone planning to specialize in these items. Written by Richard and Barbara Reddock, the book contains background history as well as illustrations of Mr. Peanut items. Prices are also included.

All the salt and peppers pictured here were wrapper premiums. They are still relatively easy to find. In addition to being offered as a premium, the sets could also be purchased in Planters Peanuts Shops. All the items shown were made in the United States and date from the 1930's to the present.

Row 1: (1) $22.00-25.00 (2) $22.00-25.00 (3) $15.00-20.00 (4) $15.00-18.00 (5) $22.00-25.00

Row 2: (1) $22.00-25.00 (2) $15.00-18.00 (3) $18.00-20.00 (4) $15.00-18.00 (5) $22.00-25.00 (6) $22.00-25.00

Row 3: (1) $12.00-15.00 (2) $12.00-15.00 (3) $12.00-15.00

Row 4: All Sets $8.00-10.00

Row 5: (1) $8.00-10.00   (2) $8.00-10.00   (3) $8.00-10.00   (4) $15.00-20.00

Animals: Animal Carriers

Now, here are some very strange sets. Purple cows, yellow poodles, pink elephants. What next! How about a reindeer with rabbits, a rooster carrying suitcases or cats and dogs with buckets and baskets. In the shaker world, wonders never cease.

If one started a collection of the most bizarre shakers, this is undoubtedly the best place to start. Heading the list would be the yellow poodle and the purple cows... with the rooster not far behind. Adding to the strangeness is the fact that, in some cases, the largest piece serves as nothing more than a holder for the salt and pepper shakers. Some of them are large enough to have served as sugar bowls at the very least.

The pink elephant, however, is an exception to this observation. He carries a vinegar and oil cruet (quite happily it seems) in addition to the shakers. The donkey set also has cruets as well as salt and peppers.

It is almost with a sense of relief that one sees the little black and white cow, quite normal looking, with milk can shakers. It is small enough to be included in a general collection without being conspicuous--which certainly can't be said for the others on this page.

The sets pictured on this page are either ceramic or red clay covered with the usual shiny black or dark brown glaze. All were made in Japan and date from the 1940's and early 1950's.

Row 1: (1) $15.00-18.00   (2) $12.00-15.00   (3) $12.00-15.00

Row 2: All Sets $8.00-10.00

Row 3: (3) $12.00-15.00   (2) $8.00-10.00   (3) $8.00-10.00

Row 4: (4) $10.00-12.00   (2) $6.00-8.00   (3) $10.00-12.00

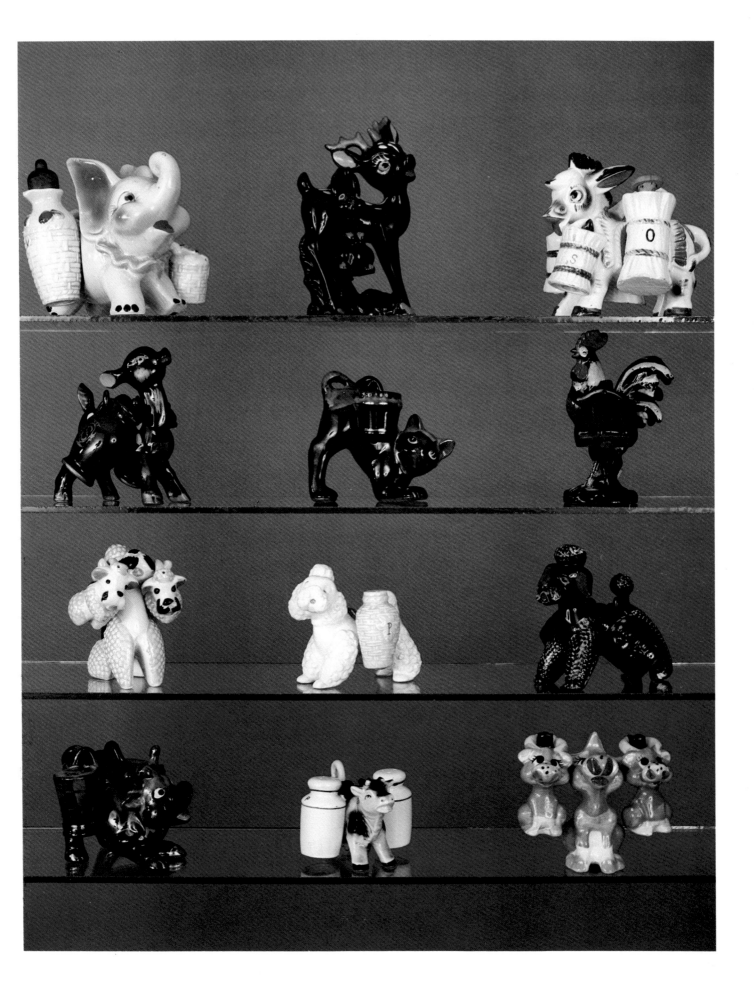

Animals: Cats and Kittens

No need to fill the litter box for these little beauties. Just fill them up with salt and pepper and they will be happy. Cats are the favorite house pets of many people and the selection to be found in shaker form is unlimited. Since they are not hard to find, you can easily collect an amusing assortment. The ceramic sets on the first three rows, which were all made in Japan, give some indication of the variety to be found.

The selection of Black Cats on the last two shelves form an interesting collectible area of its own. In the 1950's an entire line of Black Cat kitchenware was produced and one can find teapots, spice sets, condiment sets, sugar and creamers as well as other items. If you are not superstitious, a good selection of Black Cat ware can certainly enhance the decor of an otherwise dull kitchen.

The Black Cat sets all have a red clay base. Although England is famous for the production of red clay pieces, all the sets shown here were made in Japan. Prices on these sets are rapidly rising, but they are still fairly easy to find. With a little luck and a lot of persistance, you can spot them at garage sales and flea markets--and add a lot of charm to your collection.

Row 1: (1) $5.00-7.00	(2) $4.00-6.00	(3) $5.00-7.00
Row 2: (1) $6.00-8.00	(2) $4.00-6.00	(3) $10.00-12.00
Row 3: (1) $3.00-5.00	(2) $10.00-12.00	(3) $30.00-35.00
Row 4: All Sets $8.00-10.00		
Row 5: $10.00-12.00		

Animals: Chickens and Ducks

For some reason, chicken salt and peppers are very popular with collectors. There are many varieties available which are often included with farm animal collections.

I recall that years ago, almost everyone in the neighborhood had chickens in little coops behind the houses. Collecting eggs was always a fun thing for us to do. On the chickens' "Day of the Doom," we chased them with a box. When caught, we would raise the box just high enough for the poor thing to stick her head out and ZAP . . . went her head. Well, it IS the truth.

Years ago, when the little colored "peeps" were legal, we used to keep them until they were full grown. We also had baby ducks. I remember my brother's desperate attempt to save one of our full-grown pet ducks from the hatchet. He held the duck in his arms and ran full tilt across the yard, looking back to see if the man who was going to chop off the duck's head was close. In doing so, he accidentally stepped on the end of a rake whick flew up, hit my brother in the head and knocked him out cold. When he recovered consciousness, the unfortunate duck was already gone. My brother never again spoke to the "executioner."

Well, so much for that! The three sets of chickens (all with heads) which are in the second row are exceptionally colorful and meticulously hand-painted. They are from the very early 1930's and were made in Japan. Although there are many of this type of set to be found, they are nonetheless very desirable.

In the third row, the pair of black hens are highly glazed and are made of red clay. The chicks coming out of the egg in the center are an extremely nice set. On the last shelf, the first pair of ducks was made in Czechoslovakia and shows the characteristic style of Czech ceramics. The second and the fourth set of ducks are hand-painted in vividly realistic colors. The large set of white swans is bone china.

Unless otherwise specified, all the sets pictured here are ceramic and again all are made in Japan before 1960. And in case some of you readers happen to be city folk, "peeps" are baby chicks to us old-timers.

Row 1: (1) $10.00-12.00	(2) $10.00-12.00	(3) $8.00-10.00	
Row 2: (1) $12.00-15.00	(2) $15.00-18.00	(3) $12.00-15.00	
Row 3: (1) $3.00-5.00	(2) $8.00-10.00	(3) $3.00-5.00	
Row 4: (1) $5.00-7.00	(2) $6.00-8.00	(3) $5.00-7.00	(4) $5.00-7.00

Animals: Comic Type

Here we find an assortment of animals all dressed up, ready to relax or step out on the town. The little gray mice on the top row seem to be in a romantic mood! The "Sherlock" birds in the same row appear to be keeping an eye on the mice and the fireman and doctor chipmunks at the end are "on call" . . .

The brightly colored birds in the second row would be an amusing and spritely addition to any collection. The ducks in the third row are also very appealing. The yellow ones with graduation caps look like they have just barely made it through grade school! The last set is especially charming and brightly hand-painted.

The first set of turtles look as though they are waiting for a rather dumb rabbit to come along for a race; the third set look as if they have given up! Mr. and Mrs. Pig at the end of the row are definitely stepping out . . . they are dressed to do the town.

Last we see the Easter Bunny relaxing with Mrs. Bunny in their rockers. He is reading up on the latest news, while she is catching up on some sewing. The first set of donkeys is all dressed for a square dance down the road and the last set is just taking it easy, telling a few jokes and just having a good horse laugh.

All of these sets make up a delightful collection. Who knows what the animals do when people aren't around?? Maybe they do have a wardrobe and a few night spots they visit . . .

All these shakers are ceramic and from Japan. The majority of the sets date from the late 1930's while some of the newer ones were available in the mid-1950's.

Row 1: (1) $3.00-5.00	(2) $5.00-7.00	(3) $6.00-8.00	(4) $5.00-7.00	(5) $8.00-10.00
Row 2: (1) $4.00-6.00	(2) $6.00-8.00	(3) $6.00-8.00	(4) $4.00-6.00	
Row 3: (1) $7.00-9.00	(2) $7.00-9.00	(3) $7.00-9.00	(4) $8.00-10.00	
Row 4: (1) $7.00-9.00	(2) $7.00-9.00	(3) $8.00-10.00	(4) $10.00-12.00	
Row 5: (1) $18.00-20.00	(2) $3.00-5.00	(3) $15.00-18.00	(4) $8.00-10.00	

Animals: Dachshunds

This page is a great example of a collection made up of a specific breed of a dog, a combination of naturalistic dachshunds as well as comic ones. "Ernie's Pigs" from page 32 reside in the same china closet as the dachshunds on this page, which were borrowed from my neighbor Elvia. The inspiration for Elvia's collection was triggered by her three wonderful living pet doxies--another way collections begin!

The first set pictured looks very much like her own pets, but most of the remaining sets exaggerate the length of the dachshund. Both shakers on the second shelf are one-piece--heads for salt, tails for pepper. The sets on the third row are rather large and are split in half to make two shakers. The bottom row features more comical sets. Could the doghouse be too small for the first fellow? The second one thinks he has found a new friend--won't he be surprised! And the last set is a brutal attack on the poor dachshund, for he has been converted into a hot dog. Notice the bun around his middle and the yellow mustard. He would never last long at a Steelers game!

With the exception of the two sets in the third row which are made from red clay, all the sets are ceramic, Japanese, and date from the mid-1940's to the mid-1960's.

Row 1: (1) $8.00-10.00   (2) $4.00-6.00   (3) $8.00-10.00

Row 2: All Sets $8.00-10.00

Row 3: All Sets $8.00-10.00

Row 4: (1) $5.00-7.00   (2) $6.00-8.00   (3) $4.00-6.00

Animals: Donkey Carriers

If you plan to collect carrier sets of this type, you will need to have a lot of room because they are not only large in size, but there are also so many of them to collect! Windows with wide sills make a perfect place to display these sets.

Donkey carriers are found with baskets, flowers, barrels or tools hanging from their sides. A donkey cart often carries a sugar and creamer or a mustard pot with a lid and spoon as well as the salt and pepper. Again, there is a wide variety to choose from.

The rather bewildered-looking donkey with the tools on his sides is a favorite of mine. He looks like he has his work cut out for him! His cousin on the first shelf carrying the money bags certainly looks a lot happier . . . not that I'd blame him. I'd rather carry money than a shovel any day.

The Conestoga wagon, which is hand-painted, is rather interesting because it is made up of salt, a pepper and mustard container--all cleverly fitting into the wagon. The man pulling the wagon with the heads of cabbage is also a bit different. Finding people pulling wagons is unusual in the salt-and-pepper world.

The brown glazed clay set with the little yellow chicks on each side was made in Mexico. The remaining sets which are ceramic, were all made in Japan. The height of popularity for this type of set was the 1950's; however, a few sets were found from as early as the 1940's.

Row 1: (1) All Sets $10.00-12.00

Row 2: (1) $15.00-18.00   (2) $12.00-15.00

Row 3: (1) $10.00-12.00   (2) $12.00-15.00   (3) $8.00-10.00

Row 4: (1) All Sets $8.00-10.00

Row 5: (1) All Sets $6.00-8.00

Animals: The Farm

Animals found on the farm hold a special appeal for many of us. Because of all the products they supply, farm animals create a more bountiful world for all of us. Visiting a farm is the dream of many city children but living on a farm is not a picnic--it is a lot of hard work! Even farm children, in spite of all their many chores, must have their own favorites among the animals.

In the world of salt and peppers, the horse is a very desirable animal and interesting to collect. Those featured here are beautifully done with life-like features. Mules and donkeys are another story; the sets pictured show some which look lazy or just plain dumb!

The cow is also very collectible. I have included just a few of the hundreds of different sets to be found. Natural looking or comic--they are all in demand. Notice, too, the appealing set of goats on the bottom shelf. They have both wonderful detail and coloring.

As with all animal shakers, desirability creates demand. Some sets, therefore, are harder to find than others and prices for the more popular sets reflect this difference.

All the sets in this section are ceramic, with the exception of the black-and-white donkeys in the second row which are porcelain. Several of the sets are hand-painted. As usual, all were made in Japan.

Row 1: (1) $10.00-12.00	(2) $10.00-12.00	(3) $10.00-12.00	
Row 2: (1) $6.00-8.00	(2) $4.00-6.00	(3) $6.00-8.00	
Row 3: All Sets $3.00-5.00			
Row 4: (1) $3.00-5.00	(2) $3.00-5.00	(3) $4.00-6.00	(4) $4.00-6.00
Row 5: (1) $5.00-7.00	(2) $4.00-6.00	(3) $3.00-5.00	(4) $10.00-12.00

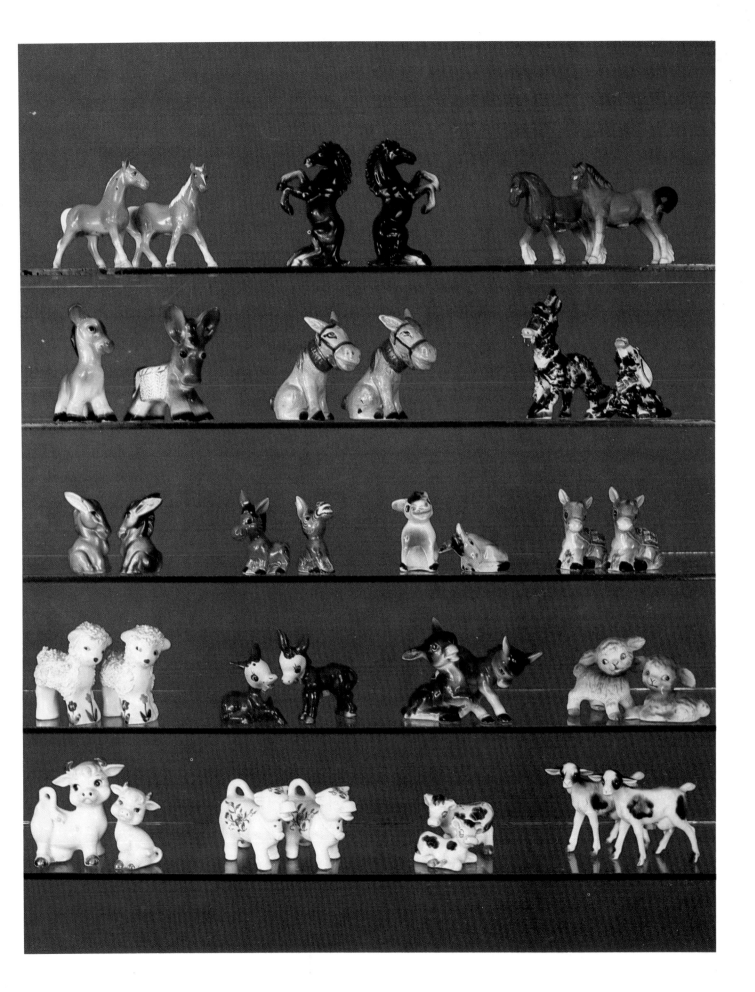

Animals: Man's Best Friend

Considering that the dog is a common household pet, it is not so surprising that dog items are also very popular collectibles. If you are in a place where pets are not allowed, collecting "dog shakers" may be an appealing alternative . . . and you won't have to feed or walk them!

I have never seen anything with more of a "take me home" look than the dogs and puppies on the next page. The first dog in the basket is a little pathetic. He has already lost an ear and broken his leg trying to get out. The other little fellow Jiggs (as he is known around here) would steal anyone's heart and what presents a more natural pair than the set in the center: a boy with his dog. In Row Two we find dogs doing the things that dogs do--watering a fireplug, playing with a slipper and, of course, sleeping. The sets in the third row are very realistic and therefore always desirable.

The shakers in Row Five are all very bright, colorful and rather amusing. The large yellow ones with the fork and spoon and the rather precariously balanced cup and saucer are great! They may have been from a children's story, bu they certainly look like a take-off of Disney's Pluto. Let me know, please, if you have any information about this set!

Few people could pass up this selection. One of the challenges of collecting dogs is to find at least one set of every breed listed in the encyclopedia--I think it CAN be done and would make an extremely interesting collection.

All the sets pictured are pre-1960 and were made in Japan. The last set on the top row and the first two sets on the third shelf are porcelain. The others are ceramic.

Row 1: (1) $18.00-20.00   (2) $18.00-20.00   (3) $15.00-18.00

Row 2: (1) $6.00-8.00   (2) $8.00-10.00   (3) $6.00-8.00

Row 3: (1) $10.00-12.00   (2) $8.00-10.00   (3) $6.00-8.00

Row 4: (1) $4.00-6.00   (2) $12.00-15.00   (3) $4.00-6.00

Row 5: (1) $15.00-18.00   (2) $12.00-15.00   (3) $35.00-40.00

Animals: The Pig

The most collectible of all farm animals is the pig. Since he loves to collect them, my neighbor has "fallen heir" to all the pigs I once had. All the sets pictured on this page, therefore, are known as "Ernie's Pigs." They are delightful with a never-ending selection to choose from.

The first set in Row One is made of bone china. They are the smallest set on the page and really cute. The third set in the first row are piggy-backs. The bottom one has a flat surface on his back (he is in a bending-over position) and the other one sits very comfortably on top.

The second set in Row Two is ready for the "Pig Polka" with music provided by the last set on the top shelf. Although the gold pigs appear to be Shawnee's set of smiling pigs, they are not--they are marked "Japan."

The popular sets in the third row are so natural looking that if you get close enough to them, I swear you can hear them grunt!

The chefs look very jolly--I'm sure they *never* have pork on the menu!! The mother feeding her baby looks SO contented; the bisque set, last in the fourth row, is very appealing, although a little newer than the other sets.

The sets in the last row are a little larger than the others. The blue ones have rhinestone eyes that would create instant havoc if one fell into your salad. The middle set is very special. It was made here in Pittsburgh by Trish Ceramics, especially for its keeper.

With the exception of the bone china, bisque and Trish Ceramic sets, all these shakers are ceramic, pre-1960, and made in Japan.

Row 1: (1) $8.00-10.00	(2) $4.00-6.00	(3) $8.00-10.00	(4) $6.00-8.00
Row 2: (1) $4.00-6.00	(2) $8.00-10.00	(3) $6.00-8.00	(4) $6.00-8.00
Row 3: (1) $8.00-10.00	(2) $10.00-12.00	(3) $6.00-8.00	
Row 4: (1) $6.00-8.00	(2) $12.00-15.00	(3) $3.00-5.00	(4) $8.00-10.00
Row 5: (1) $6.00-8.00	(2) $10.00-12.00	(3) $7.00-9.00	

Animals: Rabbits and Mice

Rabbits are a favorite of many people. I guess that when you consider Bugs Bunny or the Easter Bunny, there is good reason for their popularity. Anyway, they always look as though they are waiting to hear some good news.

The third set on the top shelf is the oldest set on the page, ca. 1940. It is porcelain and painted in a gold luster. The fact that both rabbits are just a little cross-eyed adds to their appeal. The first set in the top row has glued-on red eyes--another hazard! The only realistic rabbits are the gray and white ones in the center of the second row. The others are all rather comical.

The rabbits are adorable, but the mice are my favorite. I haven't had the urge to catch any lately, but it was one of my best pastimes when I was ten or so. I remember once taking a little field mouse to church with me in my pocket. The lady sitting in front of me had on a large sailor hat and I wanted in the worst way to let the mouse loose on the rim. My best friend was sitting next to me and, once she became aware of my hidden pet, made a very quick exit. After 27 years, I still have my best friend, but I had to give up the mouse.

Mice are all so cute! The first set of shakers in Row Three is the latest, made in the late 1960's. The second set is delicately made, with their tails looped around in the back. The center sets in the last two rows have found some food--it would be a real surprise to shuck an ear of corn and have a mouse pop out! In the world of salt and peppers, however, anything is possible.

These little sets of animals look great on a window sill. The variety is there. . . just choose what you like. The third set on the top shelf and the second set on the bottom are porcelain; all the others are ceramic, 1940-1960's and made in Japan.

Row 1: (1) $3.00-5.00	(2) $3.00-5.00	(3) $7.00-9.00
Row 2: (1) $4.00-6.00	(2) $4.00-6.00	(3) $2.00-3.00
Row 3: (1) $5.00-7.00	(2) $6.00-8.00	(3) $4.00-6.00
Row 4: (1) $4.00-6.00	(2) $6.00-8.00	(3) $4.00-6.00
Row 5: (1) $7.00-9.00	(2) $8.00-10.00	(3) $2.00-3.00

Animals: The Woods

Most of us have come in contact with at least a few of the animals in this section. Squirrels, raccoons, deer, foxes and skunks can be found in the woods in many areas of the United States.

The first set of skunks is marked "Rosemeade." They are high-gloss black glaze, made by the Whapeton Pottery Company of North Dakota which operated from 1940 until 1961. Although quite a few sets appear to have been made by this company, this is the only example I have come across. Until researching this set, I was not aware of this company and was delighted to discover another American manufacturer that produced shakers. Had they not been marked, I never would have known. I hope to find enough sets for a full-page display in my next book. The sets all have the same type of shiny black glaze, so keep your eyes open . . .

The center set of foxes on the second shelf are the most realistically portrayed of all these woodland animal sets. The set of chipmunks at the end of the bottom row, however, are very strange. There is something distinctly unappealing about shaking salt or pepper through real fur! I have no idea why manufacturers use decorations such as this. I can only assume they did not expect people to really use them. This type of "Use at your own risk" salt and pepper shaker would probably make an interesting (if not bizarre) collection. There are quite a few shakers of this type sprinkled throughout the book.

The last set in the fourth row and the first two sets in the bottom row are hand-painted. All the sets are ceramic, dating from the 1940's through the mid-1960's, and, with the exception of the Rosemeade set, were made in Japan.

Row 1: (1) $35.00-40.00   (2) $6.00-8.00   (3) $8.00-10.00

Row 2: (1) $3.00-5.00   (2) $8.00-10.00   (3) $4.00-6.00

Row 3: (1) $3.00-5.00   (2) $7.00-9.00   (3) $5.00-7.00

Row 4: (1) $3.00-5.00   (2) $5.00-7.00   (3) $4.00-6.00

Row 5: All Sets $6.00-8.00

Animals: The Zoo

Since the variety is so endless, collecting animal salt and peppers can be very fulfilling. There seems to be a special fondness for the animals we would most likely find in the zoo. As a child, I always found the zoo fascinating. It was always one of my favorite places to visit--and I bet it was one of yours, too. Since none of the animals pictured here would make a suitable pet in the home, the next best thing is to hunt for them in miniature. S & P manufacturers may have sensed this in designing their shakers, because I have come across every animal imaginable at one time or another. Even Noah couldn't surpass the variety of animals found in a good specialized collection of shakers!

In this category, the most sought after animals are the elephants, the monkeys and the bears. Most collectors of elephants prefer the trunks turned up. Superstition warns that an elephant with his trunk down is bad luck. The tan elephant with the tusks, pictured at the end of the fourth row, is one of my favorites. It is very detailed and life-like. Incidentally, has anyone seen a PINK elephant lately?

The monkeys are really cute--notice the one on the telephone. I'm sure he's not calling "Speak No Evil" who is sitting next to him. Both of these sets are porcelain and date from the 1930's. Notice also the tigers and leopards--they are so well detailed and are absolutely beautiful.

Since there are so many animals from which to choose, you can collect them all, choose your favorite, or even concentrate on the hard-to-find species. For some reason, the buffalo is one of the hardest animals to find in shaker form and would be a real challenge to collect. I have only one set which is pictured in the chalkware section.

Most of the sets pictured are ceramic, the exceptions being porcelain. The hand-painted ones are very desirable and therefore command a higher price. The workmanship on some of the sets in this book is unbelievable, especially since most of the S & P's sold originally for less than a dollar. Obviously the Japanese had not yet heard of "union wages"!

All of the sets pictured here are marked "Made in Japan."

Row 1: (1) $6.00-8.00	(2) $10.00-15.00	(3) $6.00-8.00
Row 2: (1) $4.00-6.00	(2) $10.00-12.00	(3) $15.00-20.00
Row 3: (1) $15.00-18.00	(2) $8.00-10.00	(3) $5.00-7.00
Row 4: (1) $6.00-8.00	(2) $6.00-8.00	(3) $8.00-10.00
Row 5: (1) $15.00-18.00	(2) $8.00-10.00	(3) $15.00-18.00

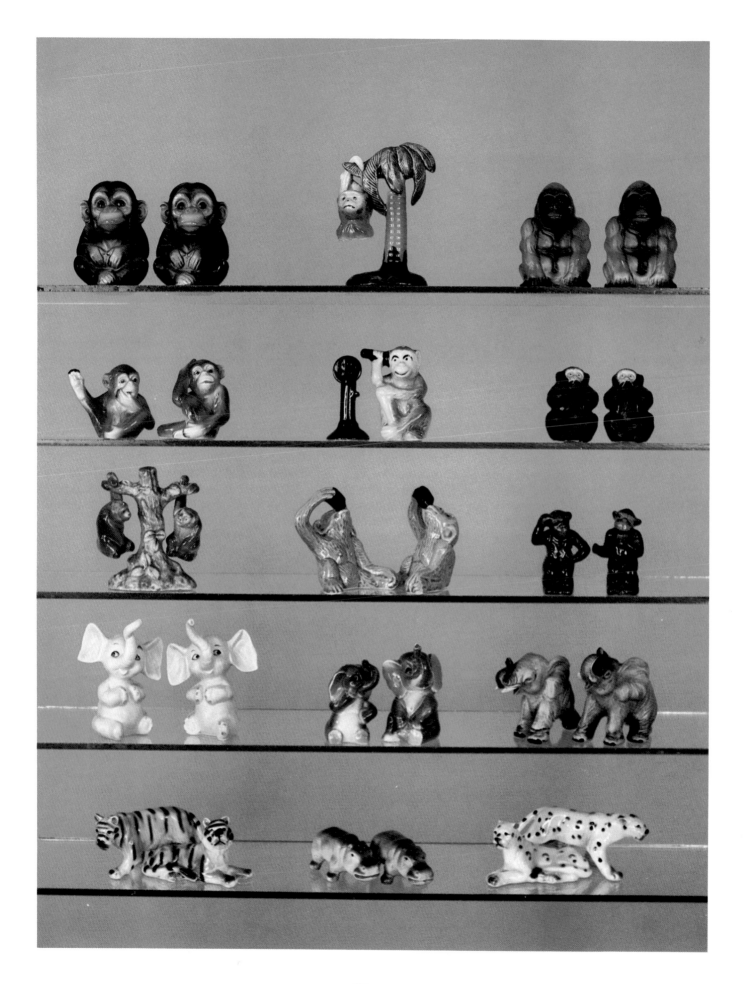

39

Animals: The Zoo (continued)

The zebra and the giraffe are among the most beautiful of the wild animals. Their intricate coloring is one of nature's works of art. Several of my friends in ceramic classes have painted zebras and have found it to be a real challenge. The giraffes pictured here with the "wrap around" necks are very hard to separate and, as a result, are very easily broken.

The first set in the last row is a pair of charming raccoons. They are a little larger than most of the shakers on this page, but they make a very nice addition to a collection. The natural shades of brown and tan enhance the beauty of this set.

The remaining shakers on this page are bears. This animal is VERY collectible in any form. Even babies must have at least one teddy bear! It seems to be difficult for adults to buy bears for themselves (although many of them do). My friend Mary uses her antique doll and toy shop as a front--just to buy bears for herself!!

It is much easier (and less expensive) to just collect bear salt and peppers. There are again so many to choose from, as you can see . . . brown bears and gray, lovable teddies and black-and-white pandas. The list is endless.

Bear collecting has been of interest to many people for a long while, but in the past few years, bears have really caught on as one of the top collectibles. Several excellent books on bear collectibles have been published recently and are a real asset to the collector. Although no shakers are listed in these books, they can help identify the different types of sets available. Some of the bears shown are toy-like, others are life-like and they are all great!

Made of ceramic and dating from the 1940's through the 1960's, these sets were all made in Japan.

Row 1: (1) $8.00-10.00	(2) $10.00-12.00	(3) $8.00-10.00
Row 2: (1) $8.00-10.00	(2) $4.00-6.00	(3) $8.00-10.00
Row 3: (1) $6.00-8.00	(2) $4.00-6.00	(3) $4.00-6.00
Row 4: (1) $3.00-5.00	(2) $4.00-6.00	(3) $3.00-5.00
Row 5: (1) $8.00-10.00	(2) $4.00-6.00	(3) $6.00-8.00

41

Avon Calling!

Shakers at your door! The sets of salt and peppers pictured here are all from Avon Products, Inc. Sachets, bath oils or cologne were contained in most of them. Easily recognizable because the company name is impressed on just about every item they produce, Avon shakers offer a wide range of materials and forms to satisfy any collector.

Part of the varied selection of glassware offered by the company, the Crystalpoint set of cobalt blue shakers in the first row and the Cape Cod set of red shakers in the third row evoke the atmosphere of Colonial kitchens. The tall black set on the first shelf would add an elegant touch to almost any table setting.

Shaker sets in the second row are all from the "Kitchen Figurals" series. The floral sets in the center were released in 1968, while the vine-type floral design on each end is from 1967. Bright and colorful, any of these sets add a cheerful note to the kitchen. The Pennsylvania Dutch motif is very popular also.

California Perfume Company was the original name of the Avon Company. It began production in the late 1880's and, after many changes, became Avon Products Inc. in the mid-1930's. It is a rare and happy occurance when one can buy and use a product, save the empty containers and find their value as collectibles increase year after year. As a result, the company is familiar to collectors all over the world.

The little figural sets are sure to win your heart. These sets, however, never contained a product but were sold "as is." The little girl and her teddy bear, along with a figural tree for hors d' oeuvres, were offered in 1979. The Sunny Bunnies were sold at Easter time in 1983. Both of these sets are ceramic. The little boy and girl are "Santa's Helpers" which were offered in 1983 for Christmas. This set is porcelain, of excellent quality with beautiful detailing. They are so absolutely adorable that I may not return them to their owners!

All of the Avon sets are on loan to me from the collection of my dear sister Dee and her husband David. This is a miniscule part of their collection of over 10,000 Avon pieces--if you doubt that collecting Avon can be addictive, just ask THEM!

Row 1: (1) $12.00-15.00	(2) $16.00-18.00	(3) $6.00-8.00	
Row 2: (1) $20.00-22.00	(2) $16.00-18.00	(3) $16.00-18.00	(4) $20.00-22.00
Row 3: (1) $10.00-12.00	(2) $20.00-22.00	(3) $12.00-15.00	
Row 4: (1) $16.00-18.00	(2) $8.00-10.00	(3) $10.00-12.00	(4) $12.00-15.00
Row 5: (1) $18.00-20.00	(2) $15.00-18.00	(3) $12.00-15.00	

43

Bakelite

With the upsurge of interest in the Art Deco era, the sets pictured here have gained in popularity. Their clean lines and 1930's coloring have made them very desirable to those who collect Art Deco items. Some people refer to these shakers as "celluloid." In my opinion, however, this is incorrect. Celluloid is a highly flammable substance extremely unsuitable for use in a kitchen where gas flame, pilot lights and ovens are all very much in evidence. In addition, even high quality celluloid is extremely brittle and very thin--one careless move and a celluloid shaker would be demolished (if it hadn't already burst into flames!). I believe, therefore, that these sets are made of Bakelite, a tough thermo-plastic material that is heat-resistant and durable. Inexpensive and colorful jewelry was also made of Bakelite during the 1920's and 30's, often selling for less than $1.00. Today, this jewelry is commanding some very high prices.

Although most of the sets pictured are made from Bakelite, some of the sets in the last three rows were made during the "transition" period when the manufacture of Bakelite was giving way to the production of modern day plastics, somewhere in the late 1940's.

The sets in the first two rows are the most desirable. They are very heavy with a marbleized effect and, considering their thickness, could not have held much salt nor pepper. The first set, figurals of the Washington Monument, is just under five inches tall. The next set is very unusual; it is a mortar and pestle set and the mortar is wooden.

The sets on each end of the center row are one-piece mechanical types. The first one has glass shakers attached to the red base. If you push the button on the top between the shakers, it will release the condiment from the bottom of the shaker. The set at the opposite end of the row is also very interesting. There is a button on the bottom of the base which, when pushed, activates the small red part on the top. This part lifts, simulating a rocket taking off, and the salt or pepper is neatly dispensed from the top. The second set in this row is shaped like a shotgun shell. As you can see, the base is metal and very realistic looking. This was often used as an advertisement for ammunition companies.

You will notice that many of these sets are shaped like rockets or bombs--a classic shape of the Art Deco period and one which may have reflected the growing concern over the World War II. The center pair in the fourth row are in the form of rockets--a very popular set from this era.

The remaining sets are later ones and rather uninteresting compared with some of the more elaborate earlier examples. Keep your eye on these Bakelite sets. They are rising rapidly in value and soon may disappear from the market as so many other collectibles have. More and more of these sets are appearing at antique shows with hefty price tags. Belonging to the Art Deco era provides a lot of their charm and collectors *are* taking notice.

Row 1: (1) $28.00-30.00	(2) $28.00-30.00	(3) $20.00-22.00	(4) $22.00-25.00
Row 2: (1) $18.00-20.00	(2) $28.00-30.00	(3) $20.00-22.00	(4) $20.00-22.00
Row 3: (1) $12.00-15.00	(2) $12.00-15.00	(3) $3.00-5.00	(4) $8.00-10.00
Row 4: (1) $5.00-7.00	(2) $15.00-18.00	(3) $5.00-7.00	
Row 5: (1) $3.00-5.00	(2) $3.00-5.00	(3) $4.00-6.00	(4) $3.00-5.00

Bone China

Bone china originated about 1800. The ashes of charred animal bones are actually added to the clay which, when fired in the kiln, produces a very fine, very hard white china.

Collecting bone china salt and peppers is, in some ways, easier than collecting shakers of other types because sets are still being made and are still very reasonably priced. It is difficult to determine, however, whether a particular set is old or new because bone china does not discolor or craze with age. Older sets would have cork closures rather than the newer plastic ones, but this is not an accurate indication since cork can be easily substituted for plastic.

The animals in the second row are all very delicately tinted and, with the exception of the rather stylized pigs, very life-like. The angel fish in the next row are also very beautifully done. The swans, however, are quite common in bone china. As you can see, several sets are pictured. Quite often swan sets were used as wedding favors and the larger pair of swans in the center of the photograph appear to have been used for that purpose; the word "Together" is printed on one shaker and "Always" is on the other.

The sets pictured are just a few from the vast variety available. One advantage of bone china is that it does not chip or break quite as easily as the ceramic sets. Most of the china salt and peppers are a bit smaller than shakers made of other materials, and almost every set has a small sticker on it identifying it as "Bone China."

Row 1: (1) $7.00-9.00	(2) $10.00-12.00	(3) $7.00-9.00	
Row 2: (1) $18.00-20.00	(2) $15.00-18.00	(3) $12.00-15.00	(4) $18.00-20.00
Row 3: (1) $12.00-15.00	(2) $15.00-18.00	(3) $15.00-18.00	
Row 4: (1) $12.00-15.00	(2) $12.00-15.00	(3) $12.00-15.00	(4) $12.00-15.00

Row 5: All Sets $7.00-9.00

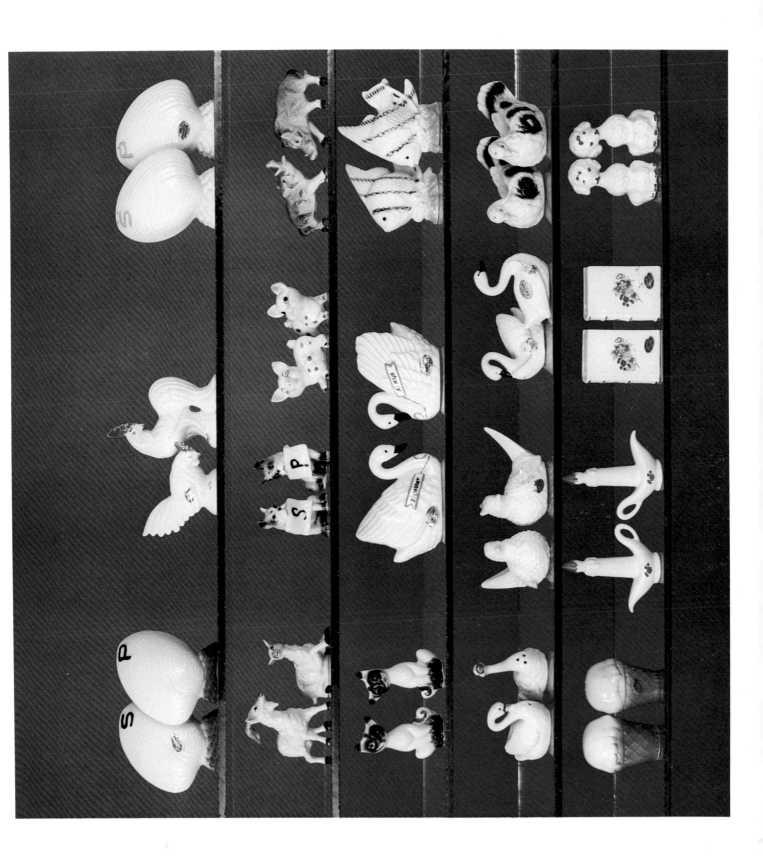

Chalkware

The chalkware sets featured in this section date from the 1920's through 1950. They would never pass the FDA standards for use as a food container! Of all the sets pictured, there was no salt nor pepper found in any of them--which, considering how the plaster crumbles and the paint chips from the surfaces, is a blessing. I do not know why S & P's were ever made from this material. They were, however, and there are people out there collecting them.

I do believe that many of the sets were made by the Pennsylvania Dutch and most of them originated in the United States. The variety is quite interesting, as you can see. You will also note how the paint has flaked off on several sets. This is very common and is one of the reasons chalkware is a challenge to collect. Many of the sets have been lost to dampness. Moisture not only causes the paint to chip, it can also cause the entire set to crumble. As you can see, I was fortunate to find a large assortment of chalkware, most of which are in very good condition.

"The devil made me do this section!" You will find him sitting in the first row. Look at poor Billikin; he looks more like he can't. "Kilroy was Here" and still is, as you can see. Other interesting sets on the first page are the tanks, radios and log cabins. I think it would be safe to say that this is a good area for collectors specializing in American-made sets. "Japan" has not been found on a single set and decals from places all around the United States have appeared on various chalkware sets.

On page 50, a roll of toilet tissue is displayed in the second row. It reads: "For toilet use only--the Wipewell Co." At least whoever made them had a sense of humor. How about a T-bone steak with your choice of vegetables? Looks as if the bear at the bottom of the page may be in a little trouble--notice the bee on top of the hive! And the monkeys in the last row are begging for money with hopes of buying an organ grinder . . .

Some amusing sets are pictured on page 51. The second row features a dog wrapped around a tree stump. It reads: "I thought I knew all the dogs in town." Meanwhile, he just sniffed himself out . . . The puppy in the shoe and the cat in the hat are kind of cute, but I find the snakes to be pretty hidious.

I gather by now that you have realized that chalkware is not one of my favorite materials. Since I cannot dictate what an individual should collect, however, I have given you my best. I realize that many people DO like chalkware and prices reflect the fact that sets in good condition are hard to find.

I must say one good thing about chalkware before I leave this section--it reminds me of the early 1950's. My dad used to teach us how to make plaster plaques out of almost anything in the house with a design in the bottom. We would spend hours casting and painting them. One of our favorite "molds" was a beautiful Carnival Glass fruit bowl which had a very deep grape pattern on the bottom. We made loads of plaques from it until the day the plaster stuck! That day the bowl became history, but chalkware continues to remind me of some of the great days we shared as a very close family.

Page 49
Row 1: All Sets $7.00-9.00
Row 2: All Sets $7.00-9.00
Row 3: (1) $6.00-8.00   (2) $7.00-9.00   (3) $5.00-7.00   (4) $6.00-8.00
Row 4: All Sets $6.00-8.00
Row 5: All Sets $5.00-7.00

Page 50
Row 1: All Sets $5.00-7.00
Row 2: (1) $5.00-7.00   (2) $6.00-8.00   (3) $5.00-7.00   (4) $5.00-7.00
Row 3: All Sets $6.00-8.00
Row 4: All Sets $7.00-9.00
Row 5: (1) $7.00-8.00   (2) $6.00-8.00   (3) $6.00-8.00   (4) $5.00-7.00

Page 51
All Sets $7.00-9.00

The Children's World

Considering the miscellany of sets on the next two pages, I am simply calling this section "The Children's World." Featured are characters from nursery rhymes, Mother Goose stories, Walt Disney cartoons, fairy tales and other childhood literature.

At either end of the top shelf are Walt Disney characters: Pinocchio, Minnie and Mickey. Pinocchio is made of a very heavy porcelain, hand-painted, and one of the nicest sets I've ever seen. The set is a knock-off, however, and was made in Japan without Disney's authorization. Minnie and Mickey seated on their bench, on the other hand, is a genuine Walt Disney Productions item and is very much sought after by collectors. Made as recently as 1960, this set has fetched some very high prices. The great Popeye and Olive Oyl in the center are even newer and are made of a very lightweight ceramic material.

In the center of the next row is a small set of Red Riding Hood shakers made by Hull around 1943. There was also a larger five-inch set made. Recently, the entire line of Red Riding Hood items has gained in popularity and the prices on some of the pieces are rising as a result. The other two sets on this shelf appear to have been made by the same company. The first set is again Red Riding Hood, and the last is the Queen of Hearts. Although unmarked, they are decorated in the same way as the Hull set with the names of the character written along the front of the base. I'm sure that there must have been an entire series of fairy tale characters manufactured by this company.

The sets on the next shelf are familiar to all of us: Old King Cole, Hey, Diddle, Diddle and Mary Had a Little Lamb which, incidentally, is made of porcelain. The goose and her golden egg in Row Four can be found in many variations and the mouse and cheese are from The Farmer in the Dell.

On the bottom shelf is Hickory, Dickory Dock--the mouse fits on top of the clock. A nicely hand-painted Man in the Moon is next. The woman sitting in the basket is something of a mystery, but she does belong to some nursery jingle because written across the front of the basket are the words "There was an Old Woman . . ." Last but not least is Humpty Dumpty, a set we ALL recognize.

There are many people who collect only this type of shaker. I have seen many different nursery rhyme sets throughout the years and, in fact, had parted with a few choice sets a few months before deciding to write this book. Hopefully, I will find them again before too long.

Row 1: (1) $95.00-100.00	(2) $70.00-75.00	(3) $100.00-125.00	
Row 2: (1) $30.00-35.00	(2) $25.00-30.00	(3) $30.00-35.00	
Row 3: (1) $25.00-30.00	(2) $18.00-20.00	(3) $25.00-30.00	
Row 4: (1) $12.00-15.00	(2) $8.00-10.00	(3) $25.00-30.00	
Row 5: (1) $15.00-18.00	(2) $30.00-35.00	(3) $30.00-35.00	(4) $25.00-30.00

The Children's World (continued)

The Noah's Ark set in the middle of the top row is wonderful! The two sets of animals are the shakers and the ark is a sugar bowl. Beside it is Jonah and the whale--Jonah is so tiny he fits right inside the belly of the whale, just like the Biblical story.

The next two rows of characters were produced during the mid-1940's and are all marked "Walt Disney." From the information I could find on them, I think it is safe to say that these were all made by the American Pottery Company of Marietta, Ohio. Sets of this type were very popular during the 40's. Since some of the companies changed ownership and/or sold molds to other companies (also changing ownership and selling molds), it is a little uncertain as to who really manufactured some of the sets. In case you don't recognize the characters, the first and last sets on the second shelf are Donald Duck; Pluto is in the center. In the next row, the first and last sets are Dumbo and in the center are Mickey and Minnie. All of these sets are a heavy white pottery, hand-decorated over the glaze so that paint chipping and wear are common. Most of these Disney shakers had matching cookie jars at one time.

In the fourth row, the gingerbread boy and girl at each end are shakers and the piece in the center is a napkin holder. This is a newer set, made around 1970. The last row consists of a ladybug on a flower, an elderly sheep sitting in a rocker (possibly from Through the Looking Glass), the Barber and the Pig and an apple with the inevitable worm.

Unless mentioned, all the sets were made in Japan and date mostly from the 1940-1950 period.

Row 1: (1) $18.00-20.00	(2) $35.00-40.00	(3) $35.00-40.00	
Row 2: (1) $20.00-25.00	(2) $18.00-20.00	(3) $20.00-25.00	
Row 3: (1) $18.00-20.00	(2) $20.00-25.00	(3) $18.00-20.00	
Row 4: Set $12.00-15.00			
Row 5: (1) $12.00-15.00	(2) $15.00-18.00	(3) $25.00-30.00	(4) $18.00-20.00

Fine Feathered Friends

If you plan to collect bird shakers, a little background information can make your collection a lot more interesting. There are at least 9,000 different species of birds known to man and North America provides a home for about 700 of these. Although most birds can fly, the penguin, ostrich and a few other large species are completely flightless. The structure of a bird--its beak, arrangement of feathers, type of claw, etc. --plays a significant role in its feeding habits and survival tactics. They range in size from the eight foot ostrich to the two inch hummingbird. There are birds that weigh nearly 300 pounds and other that weigh less than an ounce. The variations in the bird kingdom are endless.

Although the variety in the world of salt and pepper shakers does not quite cover 9,000 species, there is a good selection. Songbirds, game and sport birds, birds of prey and water and shore birds are all represented. The birds pictured on the first page are among the most beautiful I have ever seen. Many are in their nests or perching on tree branches, surrounded by a natural setting.

You will notice that a cat is after the bird in two of the sets. The blackbird with the two baby birds in the nest is so colorful, yet it is realistic. Sets like these are a delight to own. The work is so finely done and so well researched that it is possible to identify many of the species presented in these shakers. Since knowing something about what you collect always makes it more enjoyable and since there is so much to be learned about these little feathered beauties, additional information can be obtained from the National Audubon Society or the United States Fish and Wildlife Service.

All the sets pictured on this page were made in Japan from the 1930's until now; are all ceramic and mostly hand-painted.

Row 1: (1) $12.00-15.00	(2) $18.00-20.00	(3) $22.00-25.00
Row 2: (1) $12.00-15.00	(2) $8.00-10.00	(3) $12.00-15.00
Row 3: (1) $10.00-12.00	(2) $8.00-10.00	(3) $10.00-12.00
Row 4: (1) $8.00-10.00	(2) $10.00-12.00	(3) $8.00-10.00
Row 5: (1) $18.00-20.00	(2) $8.00-10.00	(3) $10.00-12.00

Fine Feathered Friends (continued)

You won't have to worry about seeds on the carpet with this collection. If you don't own a real bird, this is undoubtedly the next best thing. Of all the birds pictured on this page, the owl is the most collectible. Even in Greek mythology, the owl had an honored place as the bird sacred to Athena, the Greek goddess of wisdom. From this lofty position, tales of the "wise old owl" have drifted down to us. Incidentally, the owl, like the hawk, mates for life; most other birds take a new mate each year.

Next to the owl, the flamingo runs a very close second in desirability. As a result, flamingo shakers are becoming harder to find and prices have been rising over the past few years. The three sets of flamingos on the top shelf exhibit some of the grace and striking colors of their real-life counterparts. It is not difficult to understand why they have become so popular with collectors.

Notice the lovely little nest in the fourth row. The set of red cardinals and the jays in flight are also delightful. And the beautiful pair of American bald eagles on the bottom shelf would enhance any collection, especially since they are among the most elusive sets to find. The bald eagle, symbol of strength and valor, is our national emblem and is a part of the Great Seal of the United States. Since the bald eagle is an endangered species and is protected by state and national laws, killing an eagle is punishable by fine and/or imprisonment.

Again, many of the sets are hand-painted. The third set in the fourth row is bone china; all the rest are ceramic and all the sets were made in Japan.

Row 1: (1) $15.00-18.00	(2) $18.00-20.00	(3) $15.00-18.00	
Row 2: All Sets $6.00-8.00			
Row 3: (1) $8.00-10.00	(2) $4.00-6.00	(3) $5.00-7.00	(4) $8.00-10.00
Row 4: (1) $4.00-6.00	(2) $8.00-10.00	(3) $6.00-8.00	
Row 5: (1) $8.00-10.00	(2) $10.00-12.00	(3) $6.00-8.00	

Fruits, Vegetables and Other Delicacies

"An apple a day . . . " The harvest is in, so have your pick. Although fruits and vegetables are popular with many people, they seem to be a special favorite of farm families, possibly because of the long hard hours spent in growing the real thing. Most of the sets pictured are very realistic, and you could probably make up a miniature fruit bowl using the right selection.

I love any kind of fruit. Where I was reared was country-like, although in the city, and we were surrounded by woods filled with fruit trees. I can remember sitting in my Grandmother's peach tree, eating peaches with one hand and scratching peach fuzz itch with the other. (And, yes, I DID fall out of the tree!)

At home, watermelon was our favorite. There were five of us little "angels" sitting around the kitchen with huge slices of watermelon. Within two minutes we were in a seed battle (usually initiated by dear old Dad) and my mother is probably still finding stray seeds!

All the shakers on page 61 are nice, but the strawberries on the vine are superb. For some reason, hand-painted sets always look good enough to eat. The three-piece sets on the bottom row are on trays and look really elegant displayed on window-sills in a kitchen (hope you have enough windows!) In any event, they are certainly eye-catchers.

Page 62 consists of vegetables. Possibly because I can remember picking them so often, the mushrooms are my favorite. I can remember some very skeptical people who would not eat hand-picked mushrooms for fear of being poisoned. My Grandmother used to say "I picked them all my life and I ain't dead yet!" She is now 93 years old and still picks them when she can. Besides, our Dad liked us well enough to teach us the difference.

All of these vegetables make me hungry for a big tossed salad. The radishes on the top row, the cucumbers in the second, some mushrooms, a little raw cauliflower, tomatoes and a sliver of green pepper . . . Don't forget the lettuce from the last page! What! No onion? Well, so much for our salad.

Many of the vegetables on this page are porcelain with much detail in the smaller sets. The sets are all colorful and, as a collection, would make a beautiful display. All of the sets pictured on these two pages are made in Japan--there being no other markings to make me believe otherwise. They range in age from the 1930's for some of the older hand-painted sets up through the 1960's, or possibly slightly later.

Page 63 pictures some interesting sets. The bottom two rows consist of foods in their ready-to-eat form (except for the "raw" egg with the ham.) Even our fast-food era is represented on the fourth shelf. The set of hamburgers are recent and are made of a lightweight material; you can almost see the steam escaping from the baked potato. The pie a la mode is a nester set, the ice cream being the pepper and the pie the salt. The cupcakes look delicious as do the bread and butter set, the deviled eggs and crisp-looking loaves of bread. (Incidentally, these food shakers make great items for a child's playhouse.) With the exception of the hamburger set, which was made in Taiwan, all the sets pictured here are nicely painted ceramic from Japan and are from the 1940-1950's.

Page 61

Row 1: (1) $8.00-10.00	(2) $8.00-10.00	(3) $3.00-5.00
Row 2: (1) $5.00-7.00	(2) $6.00-8.00	(3) $5.00-7.00
Row 3: (1) $3.00-5.00	(2) $5.00-7.00	(3) $4.00-6.00
Row 4: (1) $4.00-6.00	(2) $4.00-6.00	(3) $4.00-6.00
Row 5: (1) $6.00-8.00	(2) $6.00-8.00	(3) $8.00-10.00

Page 62

Row 1: All Sets $4.00-6.00
Row 2: All Sets $4.00-6.00

Row 3: (1) $3.00-5.00	(2) $5.00-7.00	(3) $4.00-6.00
Row 4: (1) $3.00-5.00	(2) $4.00-6.00	(3) $5.00-7.00
Row 5: (1) $4.00-6.00	(2) $3.00-5.00	(3) $3.00-5.00

Page 63

Row 1: (1) $5.00-7.00	(2) $5.00-7.00	(3) $4.00-6.00	(4) $4.00-6.00	(5) $3.00-5.00
Row 2: (1) $5.00-7.00	(2) $3.00-5.00	(3) $3.00-5.00	(4) $5.00-7.00	(5) $3.00-5.00
Row 3: (1) All Sets $3.00-5.00				
Row 4: (1) $6.00-8.00	(2) $4.00-6.00	(3) $5.00-7.00	(4) $5.00-7.00	
Row 5: (1) $6.00-8.00	(2) $5.00-7.00	(3) $5.00-7.00	(4) $4.00-6.00	(5) $5.00-7.00

Game Birds

The pheasant and turkey are considered game birds. Laws of the United States restrict the hunting of game birds to certain times of the year, thus wisely preventing their extinction.

The turkey is a native of the United States and Central America. It's been said that Benjamin Franklin loved the turkey so much, he had suggested that it become the national bird. Think about that . . . would we have to eat stuffed eagle instead?

Luckily, the turkey became the symbol of Thanksgiving rather than that of the nation. It was a favorite of the early settlers and the Indians and now has become the favorite of many salt-and-pepper collectors. There are several different types of turkeys, which account for the different colors for the feathers. The male is called a Tom or gobbler, the female a hen. Wild turkeys are by far the most colorful, since domestic birds raised in shelters by man are less striking. Try to think of the turkey as a beautiful bird, instead of your Thanksgiving Day dinner . . . I know it would make the poor turkey feel better.

In most of the sets pictured, the male is much larger than the female. In all cases, the birds are brightly colored and attractive; the pheasants are all hand-painted and also very beautiful. The shakers on this page are all made of ceramic, manufactured in Japan and date from the 1940's to the present.

Row 1: (1) $7.00-9.00   (2) $7.00-9.00   (3) $7.00-9.00   (4) $6.00-8.00   (5) $22.00-25.00
(Rosemeade)

Row 2: (1) All Sets $10.00-12.00

Row 3: (1) All Sets $10.00-12.00

Row 4: (1) All Sets $10.00-12.00

Goebel, Angels and Pixies

All six sets pictured on this page were manufactured by the William Goebel Company in Germany. Although it was founded in 1871 and has produced porcelain items for over 100 years, the firm is most noted for the production of Hummel figures.

All of the shaker sets, with the exception of the bride and groom, carry the "full bee" trademark used by Goebel from about 1940 until 1956. The bride and groom set have the large "stylized bee" mark used from 1960 until 1963.

The Friar Tuck set is particularly charming, and all Friar Tuck items are extremely popular. Since I have several of the complete sets and the marks vary on them, I assume it has been issued several times throughout the years to keep up with the demand. For the avid Goebel collector, there are several Goebel clubs in the United States.

The next page features an Angel Choir and a Pixy (sic) Band. Made in Japan in the 1940's, the angels are porcelain with sweet little faces, lightly tinted hair and, of course, gold halos. Six of these I found together in one collection; the other two were purchased about a year later. For all I know, there may even be others to add to the set . . . I would be interested in hearing from collectors who may have variations not shown here. The angel choir may turn out to be much larger than anyone ever suspected!

The Pixy (sic) Band is also a multi-piece set. I know of at least one other pair that exists in addition to those pictured. It is a set of bright yellow tamborine players. Although the set appears to be complete, there may also be other pieces to add to the band. The band stand is a salt shaker and the "director" holds pepper. It is a very colorful set. Each pair of pixie players is painted in a vivid color: red, blue, orange, green and, of course, the yellow which is not pictured here. All are trimmed in gold and have paper labels marked "Japan." Of early 1940's vintage, this would be a delightful find for collectors of fantasy sets.

Either set--the angels or the pixies--would enhance a holiday centerpiece as well as one's collection.

| **Page 66** | Row 1: (1) $55.00-60.00 | (2) $30.00-35.00 | (3) $40.00-45.00 |
| | Row 2: (1) $35.00-40.00 | (2) $35.00-40.00 | (3) $40.00-45.00 |

Page 67, Top Set of eight $90.00-100.00

Page 67, Bottom Set of ten $100.00-125.00

Metal: Pennsylvania Dutch Black and White

The next six pages feature sets referred to as "Black and Whites." The black shaker is for pepper, the white for salt. These are not made of cast iron but rather a pot metal consisting of a mixture of different types of metal scrap. If you have any set that you believe to be cast iron, test it with a magnet. The magnet will adhere to the surface of iron--it will not stick to pot metal. Cast iron, incidentally, would merit a much higher price than pot metal. This is another area that I consider to be a specialty. We often find these sets mismatched, two black or two white. People will insist that is how they were bought or given to them--but it still doesn't make the set right. Most of these shakers are miniatures of old kitchen and household items. Some of them, however, depict modes of transportation. They are usually hand-painted in Pennsylvania Dutch designs. Since the only markings I have found say "Japan," I am assuming that they were all made in Japan. It was approximately from the mid-1930's to the early 1950's that most of these sets were circulated. In the past few years, many reproductions have been made and are available in the Pennsylvania Dutch areas. The paint has much more gloss to it, however and chips more easily on the new sets. The weight is also lighter. Even with this in mind, it is very difficult to tell the difference between the old and the new.

The detail is really great on most of the sets. Even though they are metal, they are easily damaged. For instance, the trolley cars on page 71, Row Three, have one of the guide cables missing. Anything with extending parts such as the sweepers, sewing machines, stems on coffee pots and handles can be easily broken. Since mint pieces are therefore harder to find, perfect pieces will cost more. The Black and Whites have been found in three different sizes. The miniature size is rare (not shown). The reproductions, however, have only been found in the medium size. Large sets are illustrated on page 71 in this section.

The sets pictured on the first page are all household items. The top shelf is made up of different types of stoves. The first is a kitchen stove, the others pot-bellied heaters. The last set is unusual because it is a square rather than a round pot-belly. As we look further down the page, we discover enough utensils and tools to furnish an entire Lilliputian house.

The array is amazing! Look closely at all the sets and notice the incredible variety: irons, telephones, coffee pots with long fragile spouts, wishing wells, egg timers, milk cans and kettles, coffee grinders, Victrolas, hand sweepers, radiators, coffee mills, sewing machines and sugar scoops. The center row illustrates four different styles of decoration on these sets and there are dozens more. Truly a fruitful area for specialization, these shakers are delightful to find and charming to display.

All of the sets pictured on this page are medium in size.

Row 1: (1) $8.00-10.00	(2) $6.00-8.00	(3) $6.00-8.00	(4) $8.00-10.00
Row 2: (1) $6.00-8.00	(2) $8.00-10.00	(3) $8.00-10.00	(4) $8.00-10.00
Row 3: (1) $8.00-10.00	(2) $6.00-8.00	(3) $8.00-10.00	(4) $8.00-10.00
Row 4: (1) $6.00-8.00	(2) $6.00-8.00	(3) $8.00-10.00	(4) $8.00-10.00
Row 5: (1) $8.00-10.00	(2) $8.00-10.00	(3) $8.00-10.00	(4) $6.00-8.00

Metal: Black and White and Others

The first two rows on this page are large sets of Black and Whites. The top row contains large candle holders, water pumps, a square-back rocker and a bow-back rocker. The second shelf features a set of covered wagons, a wonderful pair of Dutch shoes, a shoe shine box and a large pot-bellied stove.

The sets pictured on the third shelf are medium in size. The first and last sets are windmills. The other two sets are two of my favorites. The little cars are "old timers" and the other set reminds me of the "Toonerville" trolleys.

The last two rows feature the Amish people. The first set consists of a horse and buggy with a man seated inside. The two couples are pot metal, the benches are cast iron. The last set is an Amish woman milking her cow.

The bottom row has a set on either end which is cast from the same mold but which are painted differently. Each of the four people sitting in rockers is a separate salt and pepper set--the chair is a shaker as well as the person sitting in it.

Page 72 is a mixture of metal sets. All of the first row and the first and last sets in the next are considered bronze sets-- pot metal with a bronze paint. The boots pictured are brass--a rather unusual feature. Another unusual set, the first one on the center shelf, is decorated with the Indian Thunderbird design; this is the only shaker set I have ever seen that was made of solid copper.

In the fourth row, there is a cute little painted metal set of doghouses. The next set is a pair of the old spin-dry washers. Remember them? The last set in this row are gray tombstones with the inscriptions "Here lies Salt" and "Here lies Pepper."

The bottom row on this page features a pair of metal stage coaches at one end and antique cars on the other. In between are sets of steins and coffee pots, both of which are decorated.

Page 73 consists of silver-plated metal sets. Although most of them are pot metal painted silver, a couple of the sets are actually silver-plated. The birds pictured on the first two shelves are rather common, but the center row has three very interesting sets. The first set is a pair of pigs jauntily standing on their hind legs. The second set is fish, heavily weighted, and nicely painted in realistic metallic tones. The Scotty dogs on the end are very stylized, indicating that they date from the 1930's.

The center set in the fourth row has a fascinating history. One shaker is marked "The Duck Baby" and the other "The Frog Baby." The original statues were sculpted by Edith Barrett Parsons, an American artist. "The Duck Baby" was purchased by Forest Lawn Memorial Park in Glendale, California, from the Pan-Pacific Exposition of 1914 where Parsons had exhibited her work. "The Frog Baby" was later created by the artist expressly for Forest Lawn. The pair of statues now stand near a pond in the beautiful garden of the Memorial Park.

The ship at the end of this row would prove to be amusing to anyone knowing the layout of South Park in Pittsburgh. This is a souvenir of the park and, to the best of my knowledge, the only body of water in the entire area is the swimming pool.

Although the sets on the bottom row are very common, many come marked with the name of a state. The sets on the last three pages range in date from the late 1930's to the present.

Page 71

Row 1: (1) $8.00-10.00   (2) $6.00-8.00   (3) $8.00-10.00   (4) $8.00-10.00
Row 2: (1) $6.00-8.00   (2) $8.00-10.00   (3) $8.00-10.00   (4) $6.00-8.00
Row 3: (1) $6.00-8.00   (2) $8.00-10.00   (3) $10.00-12.00   (4) $6.00-8.00
Row 4: (1) $15.00-18.00   (2) $15.00-18.00   (3) $12.00-15.00   (4) $12.00-15.00
Row 5: (1) $6.00-8.00   (2) $12.00-15.00   (3) $12.00-15.00   (4) $12.00-15.00

Page 72

Row 1: All Sets $6.00-8.00
Row 2: (1) $5.00-7.00   (2) $6.00-8.00   (3) $6.00-8.00   (4) $3.00-5.00
Row 3: (1) $15.00-18.00   (2) $10.00-12.00   (3) $8.00-10.00   (4) $5.00-7.00
Row 4: (1) $4.00-6.00   (2) $6.00-8.00   (3) $15.00-18.00   (4) $4.00-6.00
Row 5: (1) $5.00-7.00   (2) $4.00-6.00   (3) $3.00-5.00   (4) $5.00-7.00

Page 73

Row 1: (1) $12.00-15.00   (2) $18.00-20.00   (3) $20.00-25.00
Row 2: (1) $10.00-12.00   (2) $15.00-18.00   (3) $10.00-12.00
Row 3: (1) $15.00-18.00   (2) $12.00-15.00   (3) $15.00-18.00
Row 4: (1) $8.00-10.00   (2) $20.00-25.00   (3) $8.00-10.00
Row 5: All Sets $6.00-8.00

Miniatures

One must admit that these sets are not what anyone would expect S & P shakers to be. I have never found salt or pepper in a single one of them, so I suspect that these sets were originally purchased just to "look at." Fragile yet wonderfully detailed and intensely appealing, miniatures have continued to be popular with collectors who cherish any sets they find.

The snake charmer and the Genie sets on the top shelf are really unusual. As if this isn't exotic enough, I was even lucky enough to find the pot of gold at the end of the rainbow, pictured in the middle of Row Two! How about a treasure map with treasure or a marriage license complete with a beautiful ring? The slice of pie a la mode and cup of coffee in the fourth row are mouth-watering!

The Teddy Bear/Jack-in-the-Box and the Rocking Horse/Drum pairs on page 76 are great but they may be mismatched. Some of the "pairing" was based on educated guesses. As you can see, silver and gold paint was very popular; the waffle iron, toaster with its butter dish and the ice cream soda and straw holder are all evidence of this.

All the sets in the first row on page 77, the ironing board and washtub in the second, and the hat rack with the umbrella stand in the fourth row are magnificently detailed, each of these sets would fit beautifully into a doll house. I must warn you that miniatures are very hard to find. Since these sets were photographed with other miniatures, it is difficult to gauge the actual size so keep in mind that the tallest piece shown is no more than 1½". If you are not familiar with miniature sets, this will probably amaze you--I know it did me. I found a label on the bottom of the tiny mailbox stating "Use scotch tape to cover hole." There wasn't even room for a cork!

Since there are so many combinations possible in these sets, matching the pieces properly without a few errors is something no one can do. You will notice that the butter dish paired with the bread on page 75 is also paired with the toaster on page 76. This is how I received both sets. I also have a mailbox with a package pictured on page 76 and a mailbox matched with a garbage can on page 77. I have reason to believe that the mailboxes were sold both ways. I do, however, have at least 25 odd pieces that I cannot match. Send me lists of those in your collection--maybe we can solve some mysteries! And many thanks to my California friends Marcia and Jeanne, who shared lists of their miniatures with me to help in matching all the sets shown in this section. (Although some may still not be right, we did our best . . .)

The sets were originally sold in "bubble packs." They were called "Collector's Salt and Pepper Miniatures" and the company responsible for these little beauties was Arcadia Ceramics, Inc., Aracadia, California. Since the word "Japan" does not appear on any of the sets or on the packaging, I think we can assume that they were made in this country by Arcadia Ceramics, and not just distributed by them.

I would guess production of these sets began in the early 1950's and continued possibly into the early 1960's. The popularity of gold and silver paint during the 1940's and the fact that many of these sets are so painted may indicate a date as early as the late 1940's--but the style and the original price of $1.00 per set strongly suggest that they were more likely produced during the 50's. In addition, the code date on one of the original packages (D-62) gives us reason to believe that the sets were still being made in the early 1960's. Since the company is no longer in existence, any information on Arcadia Ceramics, Inc. would be most appreciated.

Note: Prices for miniatures have risen faster than any other shakers. They are very difficult to find.

Page 75

Row 1: (1) $35.00-40.00	(2) $15.00-18.00	(3) $35.00-40.00	
Row 2: (1) $30.00-35.00	(2) $30.00-35.00	(3) $25.00-30.00	
Row 3: (1) $25.00-30.00	(2) $30.00-35.00	(3) $30.00-35.00	
Row 4: (1) $20.00-25.00	(2) $20.00-25.00	(3) $25.00-30.00	
Row 5: (1) $25.00-30.00	(2) $20.00-25.00	(3) $35.00-40.00	

Page 76

Row 1: (1) $25.00-30.00	(2) $30.00-35.00	(3) $30.00-35.00	
Row 2: (1) $35.00-40.00	(2) $25.00-30.00	(3) $30.00-35.00	
Row 3: (1) $35.00-40.00	(2) $30.00-35.00	(3) $35.00-40.00	
Row 4: (1) $25.00-30.00	(2) $25.00-30.00	(3) $35.00-40.00	(4) $25.00-30.00
Row 5: (1) $25.00-30.00	(2) $30.00-35.00	(3) $30.00-35.00	(4) $35.00-40.00

Page 77

Row 1: (1) $35.00-40.00	(2) $30.00-35.00	(3) $35.00-40.00	
Row 2: (1) $25.00-30.00	(2) $35.00-40.00	(3) $30.00-35.00	
Row 3: (1) $35.00-40.00	(2) $35.00-40.00	(3) $30.00-35.00	
Row 4: (1) $25.00-30.00	(2) $35.00-40.00	(3) $35.00-40.00	(4) $35.00-40.00
Row 5: (1) $30.00-35.00	(2) $35.00-40.00	(3) $35.00-40.00	($) $35.00-40.009

Nesters, Huggers and Hangers

Many collectors become confused about the differences between nesters, huggers and hangers, so some definitions are in order. The nester is a set of salt and peppers that has one part resting upon the other in some way; the nesting part in no way touches the surface of the shelf. The huggers have both parts resting on the surface; one shaker, however, fits into the other in a "hugging" position so the two look almost like one shaker. Hangers, on the other hand, are any sets in which both shakers hang from a common base; in some instances, one shaker will hang from the other. (There are several of this type throughout the book.)

This page consists of all nesters and huggers. The green (?) cow with the smiling milk can, the bear and the beehive, the mouse holding his precious green cheese and the white mouse with the swiss cheese are all nesters. The bird in the center of the second row is also a nester. If you lift the top half of the bird, you will find two white eggs nestled inside. The eggs are the salt & pepper--the bird serves only as the holder.

The remaining sets are all huggers. The sad little puppy must not have found anything good enough to eat in the garbage can! The squirrel has an acorn large enough to last him all winter; the monkey has found a coconut and the horse has his hay. I hope, however, that the skunk with the beehive gets to the honey before the bees get to him!

Row 1: All Sets $8.00-10.00
Row 2: (1) $8.00-10.00   (2) $10.00-12.00   (3) $6.00-8.00
Row 3: All Sets $5.00-7.00
Row 4: (1) $8.00-10.00   (2) $5.00-7.00   (3) $5.00-7.00

Nesters, Huggers and Hangers (continued)

The large dog and the sleeping Mexican on the top shelf are nesters; they are both separated at the neck. The bulldog and the cat are both made in two pieces which fit together and so would be considered huggers. In the second row, all the sets pictured are nesters along with the squirrel in the third row. The first monkey is holding bananas, the second one is holding pineapples. The bears have both caught some fish and the squirrel has his usual acorns. As you can see, they all have their arms full!

The remaining sets are all hangers. The lanterns on the top shelf are highly glazed and rather stylized, giving an almost surrealistic effect to the set. Of the sets shown in the third row, all of which have a matte finish, the bears and the squirrels climbing the tree are the most common.

The melon hanging from the vine in the last row is the only hanger pictured in which both pieces are shakers. All the other hangers are suspended from a common base. High on the list of "bizarre" shakers is the first set on the bottom shelf. Hand-painted plucked chickens hang naked from beautifully painted tree branches. No wonder people become vegetarians!

The second set in this row, also hand-painted, has always been one of my favorites. The glorious pink fish hangs by his tail in the center of some seaweed over a clam shell. The fish is the salt, the seaweed the pepper and the clam shell is a mustard dish. The last three sets are obviously hangers: the tall woman carries her hat boxes, the blue-and-white Dutch girl her flowers, and the last figure carries buckets.

Although all these sets are ceramic and again made in Japan, there is a wide variation in the dates of manufacture. The sets in the first row are late 1940's and early 1950's. The second and third rows date from the 1950-60 era and the last row, the earliest, were made in the 1930's and early 1940's.

Row 1: (1) $12.00-15.00 (2) $10.00-12.00 (3) $10.00-12.00 (4) $10.00-12.00 (5) $15.00-18.00

Row 2: All Sets $8.00-10.00

Row 3: (1) $5.00-7.00   (2) $5.00-7.00   (3) $5.00-7.00   (4) $8.00-10.00

Row 4: (1) $10.00-12.00 (2) $25.00-30.00 (3) $10.00-12.00 (4) $20.00-25.00 (5) $12.00-15.00 (6) $12.00-15.00

Novelty Sets: Household Items

All of the sets pictured on this page are made of a lightweight ceramic material, hand-painted and nicely glazed. The sets on either end of Row One are of a rocker and fireplace. There is even a cat on the seat of the first rocker! Next we have "old-time" phones, a cannon with a drum and bugle, a basket of bread and a cheese board complete with apple and a wedge of cheese.

All the other sets are pairs of household items--some old, some a little more modern--but all fascinating. Clocks with faces, old scales and spinning wheels, wheelbarrows and coffee makers . . . you could easily make a collection with just these sets. Since they were all made in Japan in the 1960's and 1970's, I'm sure some can still be found in older variety stores and resale shops.

The next two pages are all teapots and there are many, many more where that came from! Some of them are very delicate, many are hand-painted and they are all fun to collect. Most of the sets on the first page of teapots are made of red clay, coated with high-gloss black glaze, and then hand decorated. Chickens, as you can see, were a popular decorating motif.

The stove at the top center is large. The pots on the top are the shakers, and the stove top lifts off, providing a container which can be used for drippings or as a sugar bowl. The first stove in Row Two is all hand-painted in bright colors; the pots again are the shakers but the stove itself is used only as a base. The stove at the other end of the row is similar in construction, but it is done in a dark brown glaze with gold trim. The cobalt stove in the center has its burners as the shakers; the top sticks out and the bases fit down inside the stove.

On the third and fourth shelves, the figural teapot sets are more than just comical--they are almost bizarre. Imagine . . . salt and pepper shakers that look like teapots that look like animals! In fact, some of these sets are just downright ugly. The elephants are rather cute, although strangely painted, but the pigs next to them have a lot to be desired, especially since the paint is worn in many places. (Someone must have actually USED these sets!) The dogs in the next row are not much better. And how about that cook with a bee on his nose!!! All of these sets date from the 1940-1950's era.

The first and last sets on the next page, Row One, are very beautifully done. They each have three parts: the salt and pepper on the top and the sugar or mustard bowl on the bottom. The second and fourth sets on this shelf are porcelain with very delicately molded porcelain flowers decorating the lids and sides of the teapots. The center set is a "nester" with a teapot nesting into a pot-bellied stove.

All four sets pictured in the fourth row are porcelain, and the first three sets fill from the spout by unscrewing the caps. Most of the decorating of the shakers on this page was done by hand; although if you look closely, there is one set with a decal of Niagara Falls. (Wonder where THAT was purchased?) A few of the sets on this page may date as early as the 1930's, but most of them are again from the 1940's and early 1950's.

The sets pictured on both pages were all made in Japan.

Page 83

All Sets $5.00-7.00

Page 84

Row 1: (1) $6.00-8.00	(2) $12.00-15.00	(3) $6.00-8.00
Row 2: (1) $12.00-15.00	(2) $6.00-8.00	(3) $8.00-10.00
Row 3: (1) $8.00-10.00	(2) $6.00-8.00	(3) $5.00-7.00
Row 4: (1) $6.00-8.00	(2) $8.00-10.00	(3) $6.00-8.00
Row 5: All Sets $4.00-6.00		

Page 85

Row 1: (1) $10.00-12.00	(2) $6.00-8.00	(3) $6.00-8.00	(4) $6.00-8.00	(5) $10.00-12.00
Row 2: (1) $6.00-8.00	(2) $6.00-8.00	(3) $8.00-10.00	(4) $6.00-8.00	
Row 3: (1) $6.00-8.00	(2) $4.00-6.00	(3) $6.00-8.00	(4) $4.00-6.00	(5) $6.00-8.00
Row 4: (1) $8.00-10.00	(2) $8.00-10.00	(3) $10.00-12.00	(4) $6.00-8.00	
Row 5: All Sets $4.00-6.00				

Novelty Sets: Miscellaneous

The following three pages contain an assortment of shakers which simply defy being categorized except under the catch-all of "Miscellaneous."

The first and third sets in Row One and all three sets in Row Two are porcelain. The picture frames, done in 22K gold paint, actually will hold photos cut to fit the enclosure. The hearts on the second shelf state: "My love for you is ever true." The set of books in the middle of the second row must have been destined as a gift for a bridal shower. On one book is written "The way to his heart" while the other is titled "Bride's Cookbook!" The third set in this row is a pair of plump little pillows with tiny little flowers. The only set in this group which is of heavy ceramic is the top middle pair, musical notes which hook onto the heavy base. Because of this type of construction, this set is considered to be a "nester."

All the shakers on the last three shelves were made in Japan through the 1940's and 1950's. The camera in the center has been a part of my collection for many years. I had always thought that the set consisted of two old cameras but, when I was having these photographs taken, the ingenious photographer, Tom, immediately put the two pieces together to make one old camera. It is a very nice set, as a whole!

The cannon and cannon balls (Row Four) are available in many different forms but the second set in the same row is a miniature set of Dill's tobacco and a pipe--rather a hard set to find. The other sets pictured are fairly common.

On the top shelf of the next page are sewing machines, gramaphones and a set of decorated eggs--all ceramic. In Row Two on either end are two sets made in Italy, made of pottery and decorated in the familiar Italian style. The set in the middle of this row is a rather interesting and unusual set of Confederate hats.

The middle row is comprised of various types of pipe shakers. The wood-grained set in the center is made of plastic. The last set on the bottom row is a pair of porcelain pipes.

Several interesting stringed instruments are pictured on the last two shelves. The second set in Row Four is made of porcelain, with wire strings and frets. The first set in Row Five is also made of porcelain but the strings are merely molded into the figure itself. The large red set in the center of the bottom row also has real strings. Except where noted, these sets are all ceramic and Japanese, ca. 1940-1950.

The last page contains quite a variety. Although sets of boots are relatively easy to find, the black-and-white oxfords, the tennis shoes and the Japanese slippers (which are porcelain) are much more unusual.

The undergarments in the second row and all the sets in the third row are white porcelain with decorations. The two-piece toilet, Row Three center, has "Mine" on the tank and "Your'n" on the bowl--and they say I have a strange sense of humor. . .

The lightbulbs are truly realistic--another reason why collecting shakers is so much fun! The refrigerator/stove sets on the bottom shelf are from the same mold, but painted differently. The pot-bellied stoves in the center are hand-painted with gold trim.

My family and friends go crazy when they see the most commonly used set of salt and pepper on my table: the salt box and the pepper can! A good friend of mine even made me a ceramic set of shakers to use for "everyday"-- and I put them into my collection.

The sets pictured on this page are 1940 to early 1950 vintage and, of course, made in Japan.

Page 87

Row 1: (1) $6.00-8.00	(2) $12.00-15.00	(3) $6.00-8.00	
Row 2: All Sets $6.00-8.00			
Row 3: (1) $6.00-8.00	(2) $20.00-25.00	(3) $8.00-10.00	
Row 4: (1) $8.00-10.00	(2) $20.00-25.00 (mini)	(3) $4.00-6.00	(4) $6.00-8.00
Row 5: (1) $6.00-8.00	(2) $3.00-5.00	(3) $6.00-8.00	

Page 88

Row 1: (1) $5.00-7.00	(2) $5.00-7.00	(3) $3.00-5.00
Row 2: (1) $4.00-6.00	(2) $6.00-8.00	(3) $6.00-8.00
Row 3: (1) $3.00-5.00	(2) $4.00-6.00	(3) $3.00-5.00
Row 4: All Sets $5.00-7.00		
Row 5: (1) $4.00-6.00	(2) $6.00-8.00	(3) $6.00-8.00

Page 89

Row 1: (1) $4.00-6.00	(2) $6.00-8.00	(3) $4.00-6.00
Row 2: (1) $5.00-7.00	(2) $6.00-8.00	(3) $6.00-8.00
Row 3: All Sets $5.00-7.00		
Row 4: (1) $12.00-15.00	(2) $4.00-6.00	(3) $5.00-7.00
Row 5: (1) $8.00-10.00	(2) $4.00-6.00	(3) $8.00-10.00

Occupied Japan

Collecting Occupied Japan items becomes more of a challenge every year. Long considered a "sleeper" among collectors, these items have been steadily increasing in value and prices are rising. In the past few years, we have seen more and more pieces at antique shows and less of them at flea markets.

Occupied Japan items are "period" collectibles. After the war, during the time the United States occupied Japan, everything exported from that country had to be marked either "Made in Occupied Japan" or simply "Occupied Japan." The American Occupation continued from the end of World War II in 1945 until the Peace Treaty was signed on April 28, 1952. Items marked "Occupied" did not begin to arrive in the United States until 1947. Many items bear several other marks in addition to the "Occupied" mark in order to comply with the new law. The mark was discontinued after the signing of the Peace Treaty.

Do not let anyone convince you that an item is considered to be an Occupied Japan collectible if it is not marked that way. Although thousands of items with many different markings were made during this period, the only ones considered to be collectible "Occupied Japan" must carry the "Occupied Japan" markings.

It is believed that the finest Occupied items were made between 1950 and 1952. The Japanese realized that they could profit from better quality items, and some of the most beautiful bisque pieces were made during this period.

Many salt and peppers with the O.J. mark can be found in older collections. People who collected before the war just added these sets after the war, and the markings had little to do with it--if they found sets they liked, they bought them. Many older collectors are still unaware of the value of these little pieces--which, of course, is one of the reasons for this book!

The Japanese copied from Goebel, Belleek and other fine companies, imitating anything they felt would appeal to the American people. As a result, there are hundreds of O.J. shakers to collect. You will notice in the second row that there are two sets copied from Hummel figurines. These are a favorite with collectors. The sets with people carrying baskets, suitcases or hat boxes are very delicate and, as a result, many of them have been broken. Sets of people in national costume were also made, helping to sell items in countries other than the United States. The Japanese also exported many black items to the United States, such as the Mammy and Cook in the bottom row.

Many multi-piece sets exist to add to your collection, but they are harder to find than the simple two-piece sets. Normally, the only part marked "Occupied Japan" in these sets is the holder or tray. The shakers are usually unmarked. If the part marked "Occupied" is missing, therefore, the collector is truly out of luck!

Row 1: (1) Bellhop w/suitcases, $18.00-20.00 (2) Dutch boy and girl, $12.00-15.00 (3) Bellhop w/ suitcases, $18.00-20.00

Row 2: (1) Hummel-type boy and girl, $15.00-18.00 (2) Dutch girls, $12.00-15.00 (3) Children, $12.00-15.00

Row 3: (1) Chinese boy w/ baskets, $18.00-20.00 (2) Japanese couple, $12.00-15.00 (3) Oriental man w/ baskets, $12.00-15.00

Row 4: (1) Chinese couple, $12.00-15.00 (2) Scottish couple, $12.00-15.00 (3) German couple, $12.00-15.00 (4) Mexican couple, $10.00-12.00

Row 5: (1) Black cooks, $40.00-45.00 (2) White cooks, $10.00-12.00 (3) Boy and girl in holder, $12.00-15.00 (4) Bonnet girls, $10.00-12.00

Occupied Japan: (continued)

On the opposite page, the pigs in the pen are my favorites--they are so nicely painted and look so at home. The set in the middle of the top row, however, is much harder to find because the chickens are nodders and, in addition, there is a mustard pot in the center! Since nodders of any type are at a premium, those with the "Occupied" mark are a real prize. The Clowns and Indians have their own following and are highly collectible in any form. The Indians in the canoe are especially nice as are the birds on the tree branch--both sets are beautifully hand-painted.

On the following pages, you will find a mixture of birds, fish, teapots, fruits and vegetables--as well as other treasures. The metal lamps are unusual and not easily found. The tea and coffee pots are extremely delicate and finely executed--those with gold trim being most desirable and meriting a higher price. Since wood is not a material commonly found in "Occupied" items, notice the wooden rhythm instruments on the top row of the next page. The little round and square sets are fairly common and hundreds of these sets are found without the all-important tray, making them "Japan" only, rather than "Occupied Japan."

The windmills with the moving blades, pictured on the last page, met with disaster! As you can see, the blades are broken; I have included them, however, because they are not easily found--although they ARE easily damaged. Any set with movable parts like the windmills are a great find.

Many of the three-piece sets had basket holders, such as the nicely done multicolored ducks in the first row. The house and windmill on the tray are hand-painted, as are many of the sets. Again, only the tray in this set is marked "Occupied Japan." This type of set is also very desirable to the collector. Some of these sets, such as the one of porcelain in the center of the third row, would fit easily into very elegant table settings.

If you choose "Occupied Japan" salt and peppers as your specialty, be prepared to pay some pretty stiff prices. In the past few years, values on these sets have at least doubled.

For more information on Occupied Japan, the reference books listed in the back may be very helpful to those who wish to collect O.J. sets and related items--happy hunting.

Row 1: (1) Chicks in basket, $15.00-18.00   (2) Chicken nodders, $35.00-40.00   (3) Birds on tray, $12.00-15.00

Row 2: (1) Pigs in pen, $20.00-22.00   (2) Gondola/shakers, $12.00-15.00   (3) Pigs/man on holder, $18.00-20.00

Row 3: (1) Indian busts, $18.00-20.00   (2) Indians in canoe, $22.00-25.00   (3) Colonial busts, $15.00-18.00

Row 4: (1) Bird on branch, $12.00-15.00   (2) Fish on water, $18.00-20.00   (3) Flamingos, $12.00-15.00   (4) Clown on drum, $22.00-25.00

Row 5: (1) Monkeys, $10.00-12.00   (2) Scotties, $10.00-12.00   (3) Squirrels, $10.00-12.00   (4) Pigs, $10.00-12.00

Occupied Japan: (continued)

Row 1: (1) Outhouses,
$8.00-10.00

(2) Metal lamps,
$12.00-15.00

(3) Wooden maracas,
$12.00-15.00

Row 2: (1) Round shakers
in holders, $10.00-12.00

(2) Gold teapots,
$10.00-12.00

(3) Floral round shakers
in holder, $10.00-12.00

Row 3: (1) Square shakers
on tray, $10.00-12.00

(2) Floral teapots,
$12.00-15.00

(3) Red shakers on
tray, $10.00-12.00

Row 4: (1) Coffee pots,
$12.00-15.00

(2) Teapots,
$12.00-15.00

(3) Coffee pots blue,
$22.00-25.00

Row 5: (1) Ducks, $10.00-12.00

(2) Birds, $10.00-12.00

(3) Chickens,
$10.00-12.00

(4) Pelicans,
$10.00-12.00

Occupied Japan: (continued)

Row 1: (1) Ducks in basket,
$15.00-18.00

(2) House & windmill
tray, $15.00-18.00

(3) Tomatoes in basket,
$12.00-15.00

Row 2: (1) Windmills movable
blades, $18.00-20.00

(2) Flowers,
$15.00-18.00

(3) Windmills,
$10.00-12.00

Row 3: (1) Flower faces
on tray, $12.00-15.00

(2) China set on tray,
$18.00-20.00

(3) Metal Empire State,
$12.00-15.00

Row 4: (1) Flowers,
$10.00-12.00

(2) Blue fish,
$10.00-12.00

(3) Angel fish,
$10.00-12.00

(4) China w/ flowers,
$10.00-12.00

Row 5: (1) Suitcases, $10.00-12.00

(2) Corn, $10.00-12.00

(3) Red peppers,
$10.00-12.00

(4) Apples,
$10.00-12.00

One-Piece Shakers

The one-piece shaker sets are a challenge to collect. Although there are many sets "out there," they are becoming increasingly difficult to find. The original one-piece shaker was patented back in 1870 and in 1909 the first patent was issued for a novelty shaker . . . so take heart, collector--we have a long and hallowed history.

In the one-piece sets, the holes are usually on the sides, rather than the top, of the shaker. The side with the smaller or fewer holes is always for the pepper--which is finely ground. Salt, being coarser and used in greater quantities, is contained in the side with larger and/or more holes.

The Dutch couples on the first shelf are from the same mold but the sets are painted differently. The set on the left is brightly painted in natural colors, while the set on the right is done in Delft-like blue and white. If you like collecting unusual items, take a long look at the dancing bananas in the center of the shelf. They are great!

In the second row, the set in the center rests on a balance bar, allowing the little bears to rock back and forth. The first set in the third row is a pair of very colorful Art Deco dogs with an almost "robot" quality, while the long one-piece shakers are comical, to say the least. The dog, the pig and the rabbit on the facing page and the dachshund in the following photograph are all partitioned inside the shaker to form two separate compartments out of one piece. The black cats and chickens are red clay with a very heavy black glaze. All of these sets are Japanese in origin and are mostly hand-painted ceramic.

Row 1: (1) $12.00-15.00	(2) $20.00-25.00	(3) $12.00-15.00
Row 2: (1) $8.00-10.00	(2) $18.00-20.00	(3) $10.00-12.00
Row 3: (1) $12.00-15.00	(2) $10.00-12.00	(3) $10.00-12.00
Row 4: All Sets $12.00-15.00		
Row 5: All Sets $10.00-12.00		

One-Piece Shakers (continued)

Although most of the shakers pictured are one-piece, the telephone on the first shelf is actually two separate pieces. The receiver, however, is the actual shaker and the bottom part is only used as a base. (If you look closely, you can see the corks in each side.) In the second row is a dog permanently attached to his house. This shaker is rather unusual because "one-piecers" are usually attached pairs of the same object. He looks SO sad--I guess it would be tough not being able to ever get away from one's house at all. Next to him are palm trees, connected at the base, and very nicely done. Several vegetables are represented: corn, tomatoes and peas on the third shelf and eggplants and cucumbers on the fourth.

On the last shelf, the dachshund is after the "doubly delicious" bone--which shall remain forever just out of his reach. The last set pictured is porcelain with a floral decal on the front, and is a rather elegant finale to this page.

These sets pictured on both pages were made between 1930 and 1950. All are ceramic and were made in Japan. Most of them are hand-painted. They are great fun to collect, especially if space is a problem. And if you are unfortunate enough to break one of them, you don't even have to worry about finding a new mate for the odd shaker--there won't be any!

Row 1: (1) $10.00-12.00   (2) $10.00-12.00   (3) $6.00-8.00

Row 2: All Sets $10.00-12.00

Row 3: All Sets $6.00-8.00

Row 4: All Sets $6.00-8.00

Row 5: (1) $6.00-8.00   (2) $8.00-10.00   (3) $8.00-10.00

Plastics

Most of the sets on this page date from the 1950's--and I remember them well! In an attempt to earn money for Christmas, I sold many of this type of set to my mother and the neighbors straight out of the pages of the Cheerful Card Company catalogue. When I was eight or nine--the heyday of my salesmanship--my mother was often my best customer and I remember that the sets sold for $1.00 . . .

The mechanical sets are the most popular with collectors. On the first shelf, the windmill has blades that turn: turn to the right to bring the salt shaker to the top and turn to the left for the pepper. The base of this set is a sugar bowl. The flower pot is also a sugar and each rose is a shaker. The stringed instrument at the end of the row is a one-piece shaker.

The tricycles are really wonderful sets. One has clear shakers and the other has small round cobalt blue shakers. Both sets have movable parts--the wheels turn and the handlebars move. Since these date from the 1940's, they are earlier than most of the other sets pictured on this page. In the center, the little people are the shakers, comfortably sitting in their own little car.

The sets in the middle row are all mechanical except the pair in the center, which are simply replicas of slot machines and are recent souvenirs of Las Vegas. The washing machine is interesting: its tub is a sugar and the wringers are shakers! The mixer has a similar arrangement. The bearers are the shakers and the mixing bowl is for sugar. When the keys on the upright piano are pushed, shakers pop out of the top and when the knob is turned on the TV, shakers come out of the top also. (I have seen many people place a family photo on the screen of the TV.)

In the fourth row, the lawnmower is a masterpiece of plastic engineering. Not only do the wheels and handle move realistically, but the shakers move up and down like pistons as you move the mower. When the keys of the cash register are pushed, the drawers come out, each of which is a shaker and, as if that isn't enough, the shakers in the front of the old telephone come out when the crank on the side is turned. Mechanical marvels all!

On the bottom shelf is an assortment of small plastic appliances, all of which are, of course, salt and pepper shakers. The last set is a pair of silver swans on a glass-like base with movable silver plastic wings.

There was little respect shown for the wonderful variety of plastic shakers until recently. They are, however, such a wonderful reflection of the "Fabulous Fifties" and all of its gadgety charm that people are beginning to take notice. With earthquakes and other natural disturbances occuring so often these days, many people collect the plastic sets incorrectly assuming that they will not break easily. The mechanical sets, however, are very delicate. The mechanism activating the shakers is very easily damaged if turned too hard or dropped the "wrong way." Several of those pictured here are no longer in working order.

Besides the fact that these shakers "work," one of the best reasons I've found for people to collect these particular plastic sets is that most all of them are American-made and a delightful expression of 1950's nostalgia. I remember I had a lot of competition when I worked for the Cheerful Card Company, so I'm sure this page will trigger old memories in many of you.

There are many other interesting plastic sets to be found. The popularity of the plastics has soared in the last few years (as have the prices.) If the price is right, don't think twice about buying a set because they won't be available too much longer. Happy collecting!

Row 1: (1) $10.00-12.00 (2) $12.00-15.00 (3) $8.00-10.00 (4) $8.00-10.00 (5) $12.00-15.00 (6) $10.00-12.00

Row 2: (1) $12.00-15.00 (2) $10.00-12.00 (3) $12.00-15.00

Row 3: (1) $12.00-15.00 (2) $12.00-15.00 (3) $5.00-7.00 (4) $10.00-12.00 (5) $10.00-12.00

Row 4: (1) $22.00-25.00 (2) $35.00-40.00 (3) $8.00-10.00 (4) $8.00-10.00 (5) $5.00-7.00

Row 5: (1) $6.00-8.00 (2) $10.00-12.00 (3) $4.00-6.00 (4) $18.00-20.00 (5) $5.00-7.00

Shawnee and the American Pottery Company

On this page, the first four rows feature shakers manufactured by the Shawnee Pottery Company of Zanesville, Ohio, which began production in 1937 and finally closed its doors in 1961. All of the sets pictured were produced during the early 1940's. Once you become familiar with the style of Shawnee pieces, it becomes easy to spot them. The sets were originally marked with a paper label, and the opening in the bottom of the shakers is much larger than shakers made by other firms, which helps to identify them. Since the painted trim is under the glaze, Shawnee items are relatively durable. Sets with gold trim are very much in demand and command a higher price than the plainer sets.

In the first row are the Sailor, the Swiss couple and Little Bo Peep. In the second row are the ever-popular Shawnee Boy Pig and Farmer Pig flanking the S & P chefs in the center. The two sets of owls in the third row differ because one set has blue eyes and the other has green. The center set, Puss 'N Boots, is also a perennial favorite with Shawnee collectors. The milk cans, flower pots and ducks conclude the selection of Shawnee but, if Shawnee shakers and other collectibles appeal to you, several good books have been printed specializing in their items. All of the sets pictured are three inches high except for the Swiss couple on the top shelf, which is five inches high.

The last row consists of sets from the American Pottery Company, Marietta, Ohio. The shakers have "A.P. Co." impressed on the back of most of them, although it is often very hard to see. These sets were manufactured in the mid-1940's and are painted over the glaze, so that paint loss is not unusual.

Almost all of the sets pictured on this page had matching cookie jars as well as other kitchen items. The fact that both of these companies are American helps to account for their popularity. Shawnee is especially collectible and there are many more sets available than those which are pictured here.

Row 1: (1) $12.00-15.00   (2) $20.00-25.00   (3) $12.00-15.00

Row 2: (1) $15.00-18.00   (2) $12.00-15.00   (3) $15.00-18.00

Row 3: (1) $12.00-15.00   (2) $15.00-18.00   (3) $20.00-25.00 (Green Eyes)

Row 4: (1) $12.00-15.00   (2) $12.00-15.00   (3) $18.00-20.00

Row 5: (1) $10.00-12.00   (2) $8.00-10.00   (3) $8.00-10.00   (4) $8.00-10.00

Transportation

Trains have fascinated the young and old for generations. Trains and train "go-withs" are collectible in any form and salt and peppers are no exception. The train in the center of the top row, for example, would make any salt-and-pepper collector wild with joy. The set is very large (the base itself is seven inches long!) and the smoke stacks on the top are the shakers. The top of the train cab is the lid which covers a small mustard bowl. To the left of this wonderful train is a much more realistic engine and tender covered with a heavy black glaze. To the right is a much newer set, very lightweight but beautifully detailed. "Salt" and "Pepper" are written out on the side panel of each shaker.

The blue train in the third row is also very nice. I have seen it in several other colors. Although this set pops up from time to time, it is more often found with just the engine and caboose than with all four pieces. There are no marks to confirm my theory, but I do believe this set to be American-made.

In salt and peppers, the stagecoaches and the covered wagons are probably the easiest transportation sets to find. They come in many forms--often with horses or mules pulling them. In reminding us of the mode of transportation used for so many years in this country, these shakers represent an era of our history that is forever gone.

The first and last sets on the third shelf are race cars. They are painted in 22 karat gold--a sure sign of the 40's. Although the cost of this gold paint today is prohibitive, it was widely used for decorating china and thousands of other items in the 1940's. I still remember the knick-knacks displayed on my mother's shelves at home--all with gold paint.

The first set on the bottom shelf is exciting. It is the only set I have ever seen with a car AND camper. These are also early 1940 vintage. The trailer truck is also an unusual set; the trailer is the salt and the cab is the pepper. They hook together and are a late 1950's, early 1960 creation. The pair of antique vehicles in the center of the bottom shelf is nicely detailed and was produced by the same Japanese firm that manufactured the last train on the top shelf, and the tall covered wagon and stagecoach sets on the second shelf, ca. 1960.

With the possible exception of the blue train, all these sets were made in Japan.

Row 1: (1) $10.00-12.00   (2) $30.00-35.00   (3) $8.00-10.00

Row 2: All Sets $6.00-8.00

Row 3: (1) $18.00-20.00   (2) $22.00-25.00 (Set)   (3) $18.00-20.00

Row 4: (1) $25.00-30.00   (2) $8.00-10.00   (3) $15.00-18.00

Water Related: Fish

One could really get hooked on this subject! Since anything of natural beauty seems to attract collectors, there are many salt-and-pepper lovers who are especially fond of fish (figurally speaking). The last set in the first row is porcelain; the fish fit into the base which resembles water. The two sets in the center of the first row are comical, but the remaining sets are much more realistic in form.

Many of the sets have the type of fish printed on the bottom, for which courtesy the collectors are very grateful. It is quite helpful in separating the pike from the perch.

On this page, I know we have a mackerel, a bullhead, an angel and a swordfish . . . I just don't know which is which. If you know an avid fisherman, test him and see if HE can name all the fish on this page!

I remember a few years ago, a woman contacted me trying to locate some fish shakers to make an aquarium setting. She was using the shakers instead of real fish and I would love to have seen the finished product. The creativity of collectors never ceases to thrill me.

The "salt and pepper" aquarium reminds me of the beautiful fish we had in our aquarium at home. We children would always go to the pet store with our parents and pick out additions to add to our collection and, after marveling at the many varieties to choose from, we would select the most colorful ones. Maybe that was the start of my collecting career. . .

Fish and other water-related sets are most popular with collectors who live near water--a sort of natural affinity. The assortment of fish to be found, however, is so cast that you could really divide them into sub-groups such as fresh water fish, salt water varieties or simply aquarium types--and you would still have a sizable and interesting display!

All of the shakers pictured were made in Japan from 1940 to 1960 and most of them are hand-painted.

Row 1: (1) $8.00-10.00   (2) $6.00-8.00   (3) $6.00-8.00   (4) $10.00-12.00

Row 2: All Sets $8.00-10.00

Row 3: (1) $8.00-10.00   (2) $10.00-12.00   (3) $6.00-8.00   (4) $6.00-8.00

Row 4: All Sets $8.00-10.00

Row 5: All Sets $8.00-10.00

Water Related: Miscellaneous

The first set pictured on this page is a pair of rather dapper-looking walruses. . . but walrus shakers of any sort are difficult to find. In all my years of collecting, I have not seen many of them. Next is a pair of lobsters and, since they have a bad habit of appearing in the food sections of most books, I gave them top billing in this section. (If they were real, of course, I would have eaten them.) Next is a pair of adorable penguins--very collectible and, fortunately, easily found in many variations.

The seals in Row Two are realistic and as friendly looking as they can be. The pair next to the seals, however, is decidedly antagonistic . . . I don't know what they are, but I hope I never run into THEM on the beach!

In the third row are turtles plodding their way acrosss the page. If turtles can be said to run a race, they run a close race with frogs in popularity. Speaking of frogs, I must apologize for having none in this section. The frog salt and pepper sets are so popular, I didn't realize that I had none left. In my next book, I promise that I'll have an entire page full of nothing but frogs . . . and possible a few more turtles, just to keep the "race" going.

The first set in the fourth row are lobsters, the last set are crabs; both sets are made of porcelain. (If you look closely, you can see the crabs are looking back . . .) I really enjoy both lobster and crab but the middle two sets--clams and snails--are in no danger of finding their way onto my dinner plate. On my shelf, however, they fit in just fine!

The last row is an assortment of shell-shaped shakers. (Try saying THAT quickly three times!) Shell shakers also come in a great variety and form an interesting collection. The last set has a pearl-like luster finish.

The sets shown are mostly from the 1940-1950 era. The penguins, lobsters and crabs are unmarked; the others were all made in Japan.

Row 1: (1) $10.00-12.00	(2) $10.00-12.00	(3) $6.00-8.00	
Row 2: (1) $8.00-10.00	(2) $6.00-8.00	(3) $4.00-6.00	
Row 3: (1) $5.00-7.00	(2) $6.00-8.00	(3) $5.00-7.00	
Row 4: (1) $8.00-10.00	(2) $4.00-6.00	(3) $4.00-6.00	(4) $8.00-10.00
Row 5: (1) $4.00-6.00	(2) $4.00-6.00	(3) $4.00-6.00	(4) $5.00-7.00

Wood

I have tried to feature a variety of the less common types of sets. The large stove on the first shelf appears to be hand-carved wood, the pots are the shakers, and the set is stamped Japan. The lamp posts are unusual; the larger set is a souvenir of New York City and the smaller set is from Puerto Rico.

The clocks on the second shelf were cross-cut from the middle of a branch, leaving the bark around the edge. One clock reads "Time for Salt"; its mate says "Time for Pepper." The last set in Row Two is a picnic table with shakers in the top.

In the third row, the first set has walnuts on the top. The message is "Your're nuts if you don't use salt." (I'll bet some doctors would have a few choice comments on that . . .) The barrel-shaped sets can be valuable if printed with the name of a brewery on them. The blue set pictured is older and the type most often found with a brewery logo.

Many of the wood shakers, especially those made as souvenirs, have decals on them. The rather large tomahawks on the bottom, however, have Indians painted on the sides and the handles still have the tree bark on them.

The next page consists of people and animals sets, all hand-painted. Several of these sets had squeakers in the bottom so that when you turned them upside down to shake them, they would make strange noises. The tallest pair on the top shelf is about six inches tall, the smallest set on the bottom measures a mere one and one half inches.

When you use the chef set in the First Row, the heads bob up and down. The cats have glued-on eyes and whiskers that could fall into your salad at first shake. The paint on the cats (Fourth Row) chips off easily and the eyes are movable. The set of birds is equipped with magnets on their sides so they can be stuck together. The onions ARE cute and, compared to these other sets, relatively harmless.

The sets pictured on page 115 are unique. The covered wagon on the left and brewery delivery wagon (Top Row) are handmade. These two sets, together with the train on the second shelf, are my favorites among the wooden sets. They are mechanical and required a lot of skill and accuracy to put together. Honestly, now, if they hadn't been included in this book, would you have suspected they were salt and pepper sets?

The sleds in Row Two are odd, not only because I have never seen another sled shaker in any form, but also because they have a decal of an airplane on them! The covered wagons in the center of the top shelf, as well as the tepees, pepper pots and rolling pins, are common. The couch and chair in the center of the page are more unusual but anyone with a jigsaw and woodburning tools could go into business making sets like those in the fourth row!

The bottom row features sets that are stuck together to look like one figure, but separated into two shakers simply by removing the head. They all have cute little leather ears and/or tails and the first set even has hair.

The sets featured range from about 1930 to the present. Although roughly one-third of the sets were made in Japan, the majority are from the USA. This is all I have to offer on the subject of wooden sets at this time, but I DID at least include them in the book...

Page 113

Row 1: (1) $4.00-6.00	(2) $5.00-7.00	(3) $3.00-5.00
Row 2: (1) $4.00-6.00	(2) $3.00-5.00	(3) $3.00-5.00
Row 3: (1) $3.00-5.00	(2) $2.00-4.00	(3) $3.00-5.00
Row 4: (1) $2.00-4.00	(2) $3.00-5.00	(3) $2.00-4.00
Row 5: (1) $4.00-6.00		

Page 114

Row 1: (1) $4.00-6.00	(2) $3.00-5.00	(3) $4.00-6.00
Row 2: (1) $4.00-6.00	(2) $6.00-8.00	(3) $4.00-6.00
Row 3: All Sets $4.00-6.00		
Row 4: (1) $3.00-5.00	(2) $2.00-4.00	(3) $3.00-5.00
Row 5: All Sets $2.00-4.00		

Page 115

Row 1: (1) $8.00-10.00	(2) $3.00-5.00	(3) $8.00-10.00
Row 2: (1) $3.00-5.00	(2) $6.00-8.00	(3) $3.00-5.00
Row 3: (1) $3.00-5.00	(2) $4.00-6.00	(3) $3.00-5.00
Row 4: All Sets $3.00-5.00		
Row 5: All Sets $4.00-6.00		

People: Bench People

Imagine a walk though the park and finding all these strange people. The park muggers are sitting in the center of the second shelf. He has a club and she is holding someone's head in her hand by the hair. This is a very large set and the detail is great on them, enhancing their comic effect. Luckily everyone is pre-occupied and did not notice the bears sitting in the second row (unless the muggers are having a discussion concerning a "bear rug").

In the center of the third shelf, we find a weary traveler--he is too well dressed to be a hobo--with his suitcase beside him. Directly below him on the next shelf is a hillbilly with his jug of "Mountain Dew." Undoubtedly from the look on his face, he has sampled quite a bit of it! Both of these sets are unusual because each of them have an object beside them rather than another person.

On the bottom shelf are two sets of Hummel-type children. They are hand-painted and very nicely detailed. The last set has a label reading "Our Precious, Precious Children"--as indeed they are.

As you can see, bench people come in quite a variety of characters. Some sets, such as the muggers, are very large while others are almost miniature in size. All of the sets on the top shelf and the first set on the second shelf are three inches or less in size. The first set has a ceramic bench; all the other sets on the page have wooden benches.

Bench people are becoming harder to find. If you have the space for the larger set, they do make an amusing collection. This is another type of set that looks great on a wide window sill.

All the sets pictured are ceramic with the exception of the first set in the second row, which is bisque and relatively new. Mostly hand-painted, the bench people were popular mainly through the 1950's and 1960's. The sets pictured were all made in Japan.

Row 1: All Sets $6.00-8.00

Row 2: (1) $6.00-8.00	(2) $18.00-20.00	(3) $6.00-8.00
Row 3: (1) $8.00-10.00	(2) $15.00-20.00	(3) $10.00-20.00
Row 4: (1) $10.00-12.00	(2) $8.00-10.00	(3) $8.00-10.00
Row 5: (1) $12.00-15.00	(2) $10.00-12.00	(3) $12.00-15.00

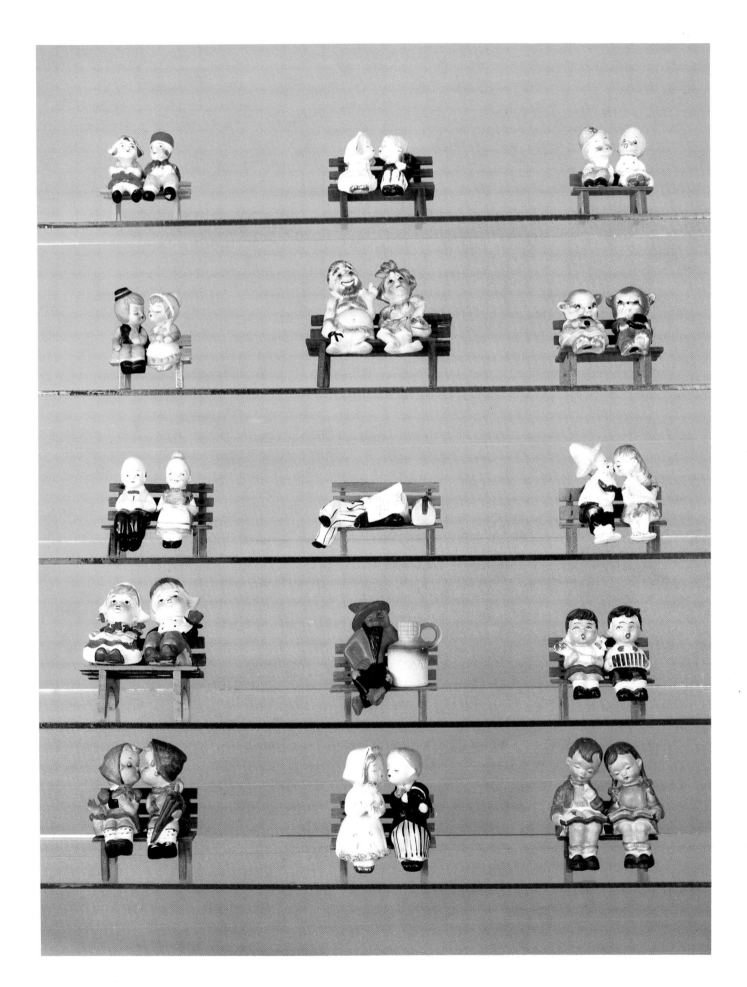

People: Black Americana

Black Americans have suffered for generations from the stereotyped images of racial inferiority that the culture had imposed upon them. The black stereotyping began centuries ago with caricatures of the native black, the slave, the cotton-picker and the Mammy. Later, other black types were added to the list: porters, redcaps, ragmen, cooks and houseboys. The black man was usually depicted along with a watermelon or bale of cotton.

Fortunately, this is now a part of the American past that will hopefully never be repeated. Since these items represent an era in our history now forever gone and since pieces depicting blacks in a derogatory manner will never again be made, collectors seem to be engaged in a mad scramble to collect anything and everything that they can find. As a result, black items have nearly disappeared from the market in recent years and those that one does find command very high prices.

The items pictured on the following pages are salt and pepper sets featuring blacks in various guises. Many blacks, however, have become symbols for major companies: Aunt Jemima for General Mills, Uncle Rastus for Cream of Wheat and the Luzianne Mammy for Luzianne Coffee. These sets appear in the Advertising Section of this book.

Of all the figural black shakers, the Mammy and Chef sets are the easiest to find. Often the molds and sizes of the various shaker sets are identical, but the colors and decorating vary from set to set. The shakers range in size from 2" to 8", the larger sizes being the hardest to find. (Size is based upon the height of the taller shaker.) The following pages cover a representative selection of sizes and color variations. The prices reflect an average of a cross-country check. Again, as with all price guides, the prices quoted may appear high in some areas, low in others--depending upon the supply and demand in different sections of the country. Most of the black items featured were made from 1920 to 1955 and all are from my personal collection.

One page 119, the second set on the top shelf was a gift from a friend who purchased them in New Orleans. They are NEW. The other sets show the different color combinations to be found in the 4" to 5" range. Since most of the sets are unmarked, it is difficult to determine where they were made. Most, I believe, are from Japan but I suspect that at least a few sets were manufactured by American potteries. The second set in the third row, for example, was made by the Pearl China Company of Ohio. Since many U.S. manufacturers did not mark many of their products, it is often impossible to positively identify the country of origin.

Row 1: (1) $30.00-35.00	(2) $15.00-18.00 (Repro)	(3) $30.00-35.00
Row 2: (1) $35.00-40.00	(2) $40.00-45.00	(3) $35.00-40.00
Row 3: (1) $40.00-45.00	(2) $60.00-65.00	(3) $40.00-45.00
Row 4: (1) $25.00-30.00	(2) $25.00-30.00	(3) $25.00-30.00
Row 5: (1) $40.00-45.00	(2) $40.00-45.00	(3) $40.00-45.00

People: Black Americana (continued)

At each end of the top shelf are pictured two unusual sets of shakers: one set is in black glaze trimmed with gold and the other set, which is marked "Occupied Japan," is in a rich dark brown glaze. The "Occupied" set also has a matching brown glazed sugar bowl and creamer. The first set on the second shelf is also marked "Occupied Japan."

The Tappan chefs in the center of the third shelf were given to me as a gift and, although I am sure that they have been repainted, I just love them!

All of these sets were made in Japan and range in size from 4" to 5"--the most common sizes found. Both very tiny and very large sets merit a much higher price, as do the more unusual sets on the last two shelves.

If a set of shakers is different in any way from the "common" type of Mammy and Chef shakers usually found, the set is considered to be more desirable. For this reason, all of the sets on the two bottom rows are very difficult to find. The Valentine couple is especially nice with beautiful detail, and the expressions on some of the other sets are very winsome as well as unusual. The fat Mammy and Chef on the bottom shelf are really great. They are old, hand-painted and one of my favorite sets. There are cookie jars to match this set as well as the Mammy and Butler set on the shelf above. Unfortunately, I have none of the matching jars but someday . . .

Row 1: (1) 5" black glaze, $40.00-45.00 — (2) 5" red, white, blue, $35.00-40.00 — (3) O.J. 4½" brown glaze, $40.00-45.00

Row 2: (1) 4½" white/gold trim, $35.00-40.00 — (2) 4" multicolor, $40.00-45.00 — (3) 4½" white, red trim, $35.00-40.00

Row 3: (1) 5" turquoise/gold trim, $35.00-40.00 — (2) 4" Tappan, $30.00-35.00 — (3) 5" yellow/red, black trim, $35.00-40.00

Row 4: (1) Mammy & Butler, $70.00-75.00 — (2) Valentine couple, $60.00-65.00 — (3) 4½" red, white, gray, $35.00-40.00

Row 5: (1) 5" Boy & Girl, $45.00-50.00 — (2) 4½" Fat cooks, $65.00-70.00 — (3) 4" couple, unusual expression, $45.00-50.00

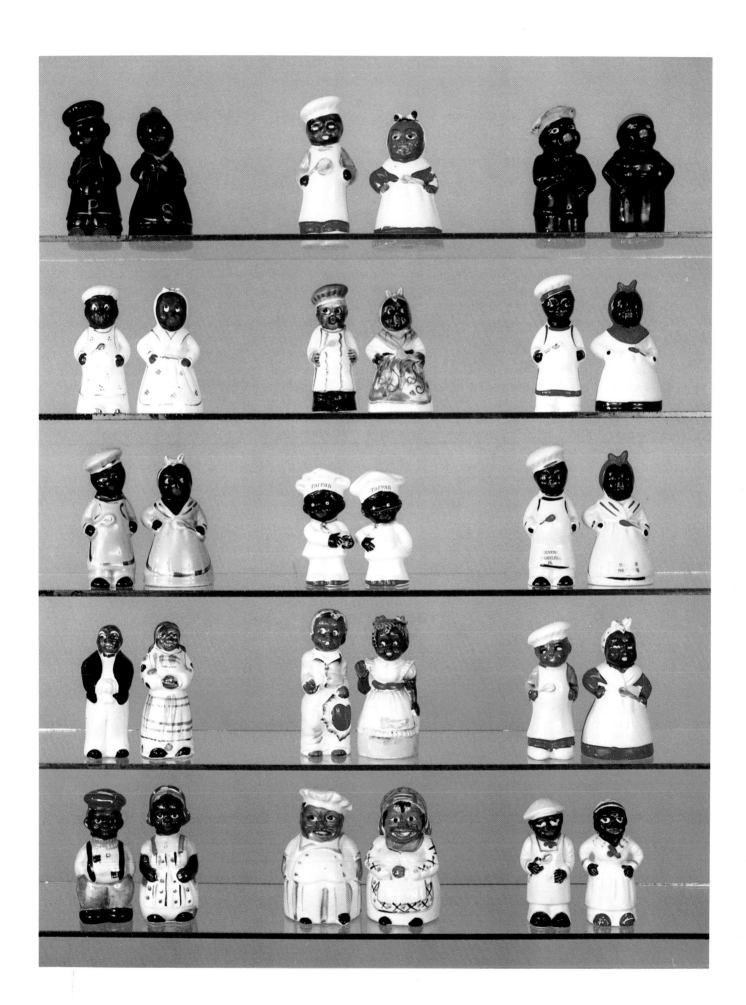

People: Black Americana (continued)

Pictured here are some of the larger sets. I believe the first set on the top shelf, which is 8" high, is the tallest set of shakers available in this type. You will notice similar sets in smaller sizes pictured on the other pages. I have seen other kitchen items to match this set and, in my own collection, I have the one-piece vinegar and oil cruet. The next set is the large Pearl China Company set. I have the chef cookie jar to match and I am now in search of his wife (cookie jar version)!

The next three sets range in size from 5½" to 7". Notice that the Mammy on either end is holding a rolling pin instead of a spoon--a nice variation. The large script letters on these sets make it easy to select your seasoning. And, of course, in the middle is a smaller version of the set pictured above.

The stove sets on the bottom are very popular. Although I have found no markings on any of these, I am sure that they are American made. The stove was made to hold drippings from bacon or other means, but more recently, they have been used as sugar bowls. These sets come in many different colors, all with gold trim and were popular during the 1940's. Keep an eye open for just the stove at flea markets--you can always match it up with a set of shakers of the same color. These large sets are very much sought after and, as a result, are usually hard to find.

Row 1: (1) 8" red, white, blue,
$100.00-125.00

(2) 7½" Pearl China, yellow/red, black trim,
$125.00-150.00

Row 2: (1) 7" yellow/red, black trim,
$65.00-75.00

(2) 6½" red, white, blue
$65.00-75.00

(3) 5½" white,
$60.00-70.00

Row 3: (1) 4" light green shakers,
$75.00-85.00 (Set)

(2) Same in yellow,
$75.00-85.00 (Set)

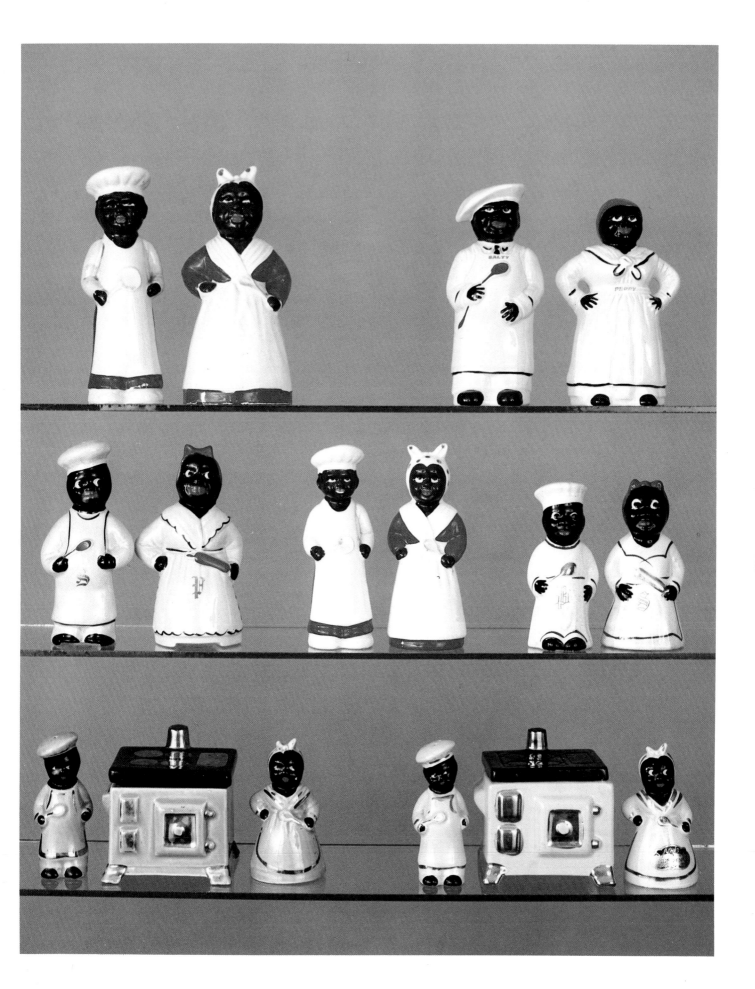

People: Black Americana (continued)

The sets pictured on this page give some hint of the great variety of black items that can still be found. The family on the top shelf fits into the wire rack and offers a complete selection of salt, pepper, vinegar and oil. Very colorful and well detailed, the set is from the 1940's and was made in Japan--a great addition to any collection.

Notice that the chef belonging to the pink stove set on the second shelf is missing. He left for a pack of cigarettes in 1947 and has not been seen since! If you know of his wherabouts, *please* drop me a line.

The large brightly painted set on the second shelf is the only one of this type I have ever seen. The details are wonderful, with "Salt" and "Pepper" written on the large plate and spoon. Again, this is the kind of set that would be a nice find for anyone.

The wooden bellhop carrying two round containers at the bottom of the page is all hand-painted. The very strange bongo player on the other end of the shelf is all wire with a little wooden head. He is holding two ceramic bongo drums. Take note of his grass skirt. All I can say is "He was here . . . so here he is!"

The Mammy in the center on the bottom shelf is very special to me. It is one of the really great sets my sister found for me in her search for more Avon collectibles. The set includes salt, pepper and a mustard container--all shaped like barrels. The Mammy is attached to the base that the barrels rest on. The entire piece has a beautiful glass-like glaze over finely modeled details. What a thrill for a collector to acquire such unique pieces--which is why collecting is usually so much fun!

Row 1: (1) 4" salt & pepper shakers, 5" vinegar & oil on rack, $125.00-150.00 (Set)

Row 2: (1) Pink stove, one shaker, $75.00-85.00 (Set)

(2) 6" Mammy & Chef, $90.00-100.00

Row 3: (1) 5½" wooden bellhop, $25.00-30.00

(2) 5" Mammy w/barrels, $45.00-50.00

(3) 6" Bongo man, $20.00-25.00

People: Black Americana (continued)

On this page, the first three rows of shakers consist of sets 4" tall or less. The first set on the top row is chalkware. One usually finds this set with chips in the paint. As I may have mentioned before, I have never found salt or pepper in any chalkware set, nor could I imagine using a spice out of a chalkware container. Because of the bright childish faces on the second set pictured, these shakers are exceptional and therefore very desirable to the collector. Unusual sets such as this always command top dollar.

Another unusual set is pictured in the second row, second pair from the left. These have white faces with black features--a set not easily found. The last pair in this row is cotton pickers. Very old, made of pottery and stamped New Orleans, this set is not only one of the oldest in my collection, it is also one of my favorites.

The set in the very center of the page is a mystery. It appears to be a pair but I am not convinced. When I bought it, the original owner believed that it was an original set. It is quite different and, since I have never seen another set with either shaker in it, it is hard to determine its authenticity. Nevertheless, the set is all hand-painted and dates from about 1940.

The fourth row is a potpourri consisting of a redcap with baggage, a smiling black boy on a toilet, a young boy on a cotton bale, and a black clown on a drum. These and the sets on the last shelf, especially the minstrel singer and his white gloves, indicate the wide-ranging variety of shakers available to the collector. Incidentally, the boy and girl on the bottom shelf are made from red clay with the glossy black glaze.

All of the sets pictured on this page are unusual enough to command a high level of desirability and therefore a high market value. They were all made in Japan, early 1930's through the 1950's.

*Row 4 - Set 4 should be matched with a seal on stand holding a ball - Not as pictured.

Row 1: (1) $25.00-30.00	(2) $30.00-35.00	(3) $22.00-25.00	(4) $22.00-25.00
Row 2: (1) $25.00-30.00	(2) $30.00-35.00	(3) $35.00-25.00	(4) $45.00-50.00
Row 3: (1) $22.00-25.00	(2) $45.00-50.00	(3) $22.00-25.00	
Row 4: (1) $75.00-85.00	(2) $50.00-55.00	(3) $75.00-85.00	*(4) $35.00-40.00
Row 5: (1) $75.00-85.00	(2) $22.00-25.00	(3) $30.00-35.00	(4) $22.00-25.00

People: Black Americana (continued)

I have a feeling that the sets on this page will send many collectors of Black Memorabilia on a frantic seek and search mission . . .

On the top shelf, the first and last sets are cast from the same mold but the painting and decorating of the boy-and-girl pair is different. The set in the middle, of two little black babies in striped diapers, is a piggy-back pair. The second row features watermelon sets. First, a boy and a slice of watermelon, a chalkware boy and girl--each holding a slice of watermelon, and a girl and a slice of you-know-what. I know of several collectors who restrict their collections to figures and/or shakers depicting people with watermelons. There is a fantastic cookie jar made by the Pearl China Company in the shape of a girl with watermelon. It is a very hard-to-find item and commands a high price. It is a treasured item to those who own one and I was lucky enough to have one for about a year before a good friend of mine adopted her. After all, I am a salt-and-pepper collector and, although cookie jars fascinate me, I can't have everything!

The three sets in the center are great. There must be quite a few varieties of vegetables with little black boys sitting on top. Those pictured here show corn, lettuce, and carrrots. I just love them!

The fourth row again shows people with slices of watermelon. The second set is one of which many collectors are in search. She is a gray-haired nodder, with the slice of melon resting in her hands. When the slice is removed, a very "busty" bare chest is revealed. Because of her fragility and consequent rarity as well as the slightly suggestive quality of her construction, this set is a real treasure.

In the last row are three sets of children, each with a special bit of charm. The first set is very well done with underglaze paint. Both children hold an ear of corn. The second set is of two children sitting playfully in a basket. This particular set is often found with paint wear--so a mint set is especially desirable. The last set shown may have been painted over. I have the same set in white. The characters look like ones from the Little Rascals . . . and just filled with mischief.

All the sets pictured are from Japan, dating from the 1930's to the 1950's inclusive.

Row 1: (1) $40.00-45.00	(2) $45.00-50.00	(3) $22.00-25.00
Row 2: (1) $35.00-40.00	(2) $40.00-45.00	(3) $30.00-35.00
Row 3: All Sets $40.00-45.00		
Row 4: (1) $60.00-65.00	(2) $100.00-125.00 (Nodder)	(3) $40.00-45.00
Row 5: (1) $40.00-45.00	(2) $45.00-50.00	(3) $30.00-35.00

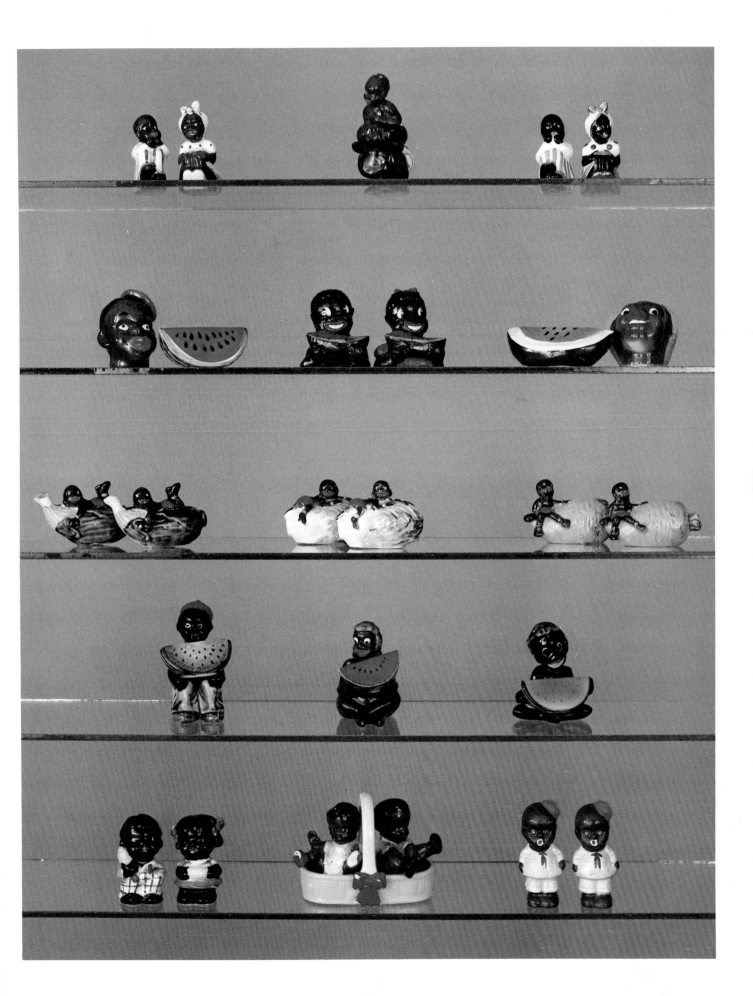

People: Black Americana (continued)

Most of the sets on this page are "native-type." The last two sets on the top row are nesters. The set in the center has her baby sitting on her back while the set on the end has the baby resting in the mother's lap. Both sets are similar in design, are brightly painted and have very exaggerated features.

The second row consists of native boys riding alligators. How nice it must have been to find so many friendly alligators . . .the last native boy even has a banjo and appears to be singing!

In the center row, a man and woman are making wedding plans as the chief stands by to play the wedding song on his drum and a friend offers some after-dinner music under a tree.

Variety is certainly evident here in this section. Notice the graceful matador playing against the bull and the little wooden pair with tiny pearl earrings dangling from their ears.

The first set in the last row are natives with baskets atop their heads. The Ethiopian guards at the end of the row, made by the Ceramic Art Studios of Wisconsin, are of very fine quality. The sets that I have seen made by the Ceramic Art Studios have always been very nice and I hope to research and feature much more by this American manufacturer at a later date. I know there must be collectors who specialize in pieces produced by this company.

With the exception of the Ceramic Art set, all others were made in Japan between 1930 and 1960.

Row 1: (1) $20.00-22.00	(2) $45.00-50.00	(3) $40.00-45.00
Row 2: (1) $65.00-70.00	(2) $35.00-40.00	(3) $35.00-40.00
Row 3: (1) $35.00-40.00	(2) $35.00-40.00	(3) $30.00-35.00
Row 4: (1) $25.00-30.00	(2) $35.00-40.00	(3) $22.00-25.00
Row 5: (1) $35.00-40.00	(2) $25.00-30.00	(3) $35.00-40.00

People: Chefs

This is another popular collecting area. Every chef you would want to know (and some you wouldn't) can be found.

The oldest sets pictured on this page can be found in the center of the third row and on the last two rows. The detail on all of them is well done. If you find any of the chefs from the fourth row in your favorite restaurant, you are in trouble. The first set are pigs, the second are monkeys and the third are cows. Who knows . . . maybe they CAN cook! The last set on this shelf looks like Betty Boop and her husband Big Boop . . .

The second set on the bottom shelf is featuring rabbit for dinner. These little chefs are so chubby, however, that they may be preparing the feast for themselves.

Collectors are motivated by such diverse interests. I have a friend, for instance, whose husband is a chef which is the reason for their collection. Several chef sets can also be found in other sections of this book but the ones pictured here are either ceramic or porcelain. The one exception is the rather strange looking couple in the center of the top shelf, which are made of stoneware.

These sets date from the early 1940's through the 1960's and were made in Japan.

Row 1: (1) $6.00-8.00   (2) $8.00-10.00   (3) $5.00-7.00

Row 2: (1) $8.00-10.00   (2) $6.00-8.00   (3) $6.00-8.00   (4) $8.00-10.00

Row 3: (1) $5.00-7.00   (2) $8.00-10.00   (3) $8.00-10.00   (4) $5.00-7.00

Row 4: All Sets $8.00-10.00

Row 5: All Sets $8.00-10.00

People: Children

Salt-and-pepper shakers in the form of children are numerous, but their appeal makes them ever-popular with collectors. In addition to this page picturing "children" sets, there are many other examples scattered throughout the book. The sweet innocence (as well as the mischief) of the very young is evident on so many of these little faces.

You will notice that all of the sets on the first row and the second set in Row Two are Hummel-type sets. They are all beautifully hand-painted in a soft matte finish. These sets are so charming that several collectors I know confine their collections to just such Hummel-types.

The first set in the center row is also pictured in the section on Black Americana, except that there, the children are black. The fourth set in the row is highly glazed in bright colors but the faces are painted in a matte flesh color.

The cowboy and cowgirl in the fourth row are adorable and very, very colorful. And just look at the little Kewpie-like figures! These sets, with their winsome expressions and their delicately tinted bisque-like finish, are always extremely popular with collectors. Since the last set in the row reminds me of my two youngest sons, it is one of my favorites. The great details on this set capture that "Let's fight" look as they prepare to battle over the TV . . . or whatever!

On the bottom row are two sets of children saying their prayers. The first set is white with just a hint of facial decoration and a bit of gold trim. The other set is in full color. The second set pictured shows two innocent albeit inquisitive children. "What's Yours?" is written across the bottom of both shakers! Although I don't know the story behind the third set, showing two children with daisy-like flowers on their heads, I am sure it must allude to some legend or fairy tale. I have seen several different sets of this type dating from the early 1940's and I would appreciate any information on them. They have that special look that says "We're famous characters"--and I'd love to know more about this delightful pair.

As you can see, children (shaker variety) are a joy to collect . . . and they don't even talk back! Most of these sets date from the 1940's and 1950's. Neither set of "praying children" is marked; the others, however, were made in Japan and are all ceramic.

Row 1: (1) All Sets $12.00-15.00

Row 2: (1) $8.00-10.00   (2) $10.00-12.00   (3) $6.00-8.00   (4) $8.00-10.00

Row 3: (1) $6.00-8.00   (2) $8.00-10.00   (3) $5.00-7.00   (4) $8.00-10.00   (5) $5.00-7.00

Row 4: (1) $6.00-8.00   (2) $8.00-10.00   (3) $10.00-12.00   (4) $12.00-15.00

Row 5: (1) $8.00-10.00   (2) $10.00-12.00   (3) $10.00-12.00   (4) $8.00-10.00

People: Here Come the Clowns

The world would be a definitely sadder place without the clown. He often makes you laugh when you feel like crying and makes you cry at the comedy of life. His wit is an art to entertain the young and the old. Laughter is the universal medicine and it is administered by the clown.

There are many, many greats in the world of the clown and we thank them all. Each of them develops his own style, although the early "greats" have been imitated over and over again thoughout the years. The early kings all had their court jester--a forerunner of our clown--and treasured them beyond their counselors.

The first "clown" as such, however, performed in Astley's circus in 1770. He was Bill Saunders, "the first original clown." In the early 19th century, a master pantomime, Joseph Grimaldi, an Englishman, emerged. He was known as "London's merriest clown" and the term "Joey's" in reference to circus clowns was credited to him.

Jean-Baptiste Aureil, a Frenchman, was a great acrobatic clown and Frank (Slivers) Oakely is said to have originated the female impersonator's bustle. In the 1860's, an unprecedented sum of $1,000 per week was earned by Dan Rice, the first great American clown. He gave the gift of laughter during the heyday of the one-ring circus and singing was just one of his talents.

In the 20th century, Felix Adler was known as "The White House Clown" because of his performances for presidential families. Otto Griebling with his sad face was one of the most famous tramp clowns and gigantic shoes and a wide grin made Lou Jacobs famous. The "Neon Clown," Paul Jerome, earned his name from having a battery-operated nose that lit up.

A definite favorite of the 20th century is Red Skelton. His characterizations are marvelous. The fact that he is such a fine artist, creating so many original works of laughter, makes him very well known and therefore collectible.

I must admit, however, that my all-time favorite is Emmett Kelley. His "Woeful Willie" has become a classic. Perhaps it is because he had a unique way of saying that the job is never done, but in his attempt to sweep up a circle of light and dispose of it (only to find it immediately back again), he spoke for all of us. The Emmet Kelley clown face is, as a result, the most famous and easily recognized of all the American clown faces.

With very good reason, therefore, clowns in all forms are very collectible today. In the world of salt-and-pepper shakers, the sets featuring clowns offer an interesting variety and are also very colorful--a real delight to collect and display.

In the second row, the first set is a piggy-back and the last set is playing leap frog. The center shakers are turn-abouts, having a happy face if you turn them one way and a sad face when you reverse them. Among the hard-to-find sets are the black and white metal shakers displayed at the extreme left of the fourth row.

Most of these shakers are of the 1940-1950 vintage and all are from the collection of Debbie Ramsey, an avid clown collector from Pittsburgh. The second and fourth sets in the fourth row are porcelain, the rest are ceramic with the exception of the one metal set. All the sets were made in Japan.

Row 1: (1) All Sets $20.00-25.00

Row 2: (1) $22.00-28.00   (2) $22.00-28.00   (3) $22.00-28.00   (4) $20.00-25.00   (5) $20.00-25.00

Row 3: All Sets $20.00-25.00

Row 4: (1) $18.00-22.00   (2) $12.00-15.00   (3) $20.00-25.00   (4) $10.00-12.00   (5) $12.00-15.00

Row 5: All Sets $12.00-15.00

People: Indians

More American than even Mom and apple pie is the American Indian. Collecting Indian shakers is a wonderful area of specialization because, with a little research, you could probably match many sets with different Indian tribes, customs and regions.

The Indian sets are always very colorful because of their elaborate headdress, facial paint and clothing. Since they make such interesting and beautiful collections, they are very popular and collectible in any form. There are many related items in the salt-and-pepper world that make delightful "go-withs" such as the totem poles, canoes and tepees.

On this page you will find a potpourri of Indians, both life-like and exaggerated, adults and children as well as full figure and bust types. Again, this is just a small representation of what is available, so you see what a fascinating area of collecting this can be.

The first set pictured is one of my favorites. It is hand-painted (as are most of these sets) and is extremely realistic and well-done. The next set is an extreme opposite in style--it consists of two Indians done in a cartoon-like style with extremely distorted features and crossed eyes.

The next four sets are of charming Indian children and are all very cute. The third and fourth rows picture bust-type sets. The detail is excellent on most of them. The first set in the third row in particular shows the rugged features common to older Indians who have survived countless rough years of hard work and outdoor living.

The set in the middle of the last row of tepees, the only shelter for many wandering tribes of Indians. On each end are totem poles, a religious and magical structure to any Indian groups. The individual tribal style has great significance and meaning to the Indians belonging to that tribe or council and, even reduced to the size of salt and peppers, are interesting and colorful objects to study and display.

Row 1: (1) $18.00-20.00	(2) $15.00-18.00	(3) $12.00-15.00
Row 2: All Sets $10.00-12.00		
Row 3: (1) $12.00-15.00	(2) $10.00-12.00	(3) $12.00-15.00
Row 4: (1) $10.00-12.00	(2) $8.00-10.00	(3) $6.00-8.00
Row 5: (1) $8.00-10.00	(2) $5.00-7.00	(3) $6.00-8.00

People: Indians (continued)

Several of the sets on this page are multi-piece. The center sets in the first three rows and the last set in the fourth row all have three or more pieces. The center set in the second row has a drum in front of the tepee. This drum is intended for mustard, while the Indian and his squaw are the shakers. The tepee holds toothpicks and is attached to the tray holding the other pieces. The other three sets mentioned are separate shakers with the third piece serving just as the base.

All three sets in the third row are made of chalkware. The sets on each end of this row are the oldest pictured in the Indian section. A very recent set, however, possibly made as late as the 1970's, is pictured in the center of the fourth row. These adorable children are made of a pottery-like material, nicely painted and very, very appealing.

In the last row, the second set is made of pot metal painted to look like bronze and the last set is made of the wood composition that was so popular in the late 1940's.

Many of the sets on this page feature Indians with objects common to their environment. The children sitting in the moccasins in the fourth row would be a charming addition to any collection.

Unless otherwise stated, these sets are all made of ceramic and the majority of the sets on both pages range from the late 1930's through the early 1960's. If you are looking for a specific subject to collect, this is one of the best. Since there are so many sets to choose from, getting started is not at all difficult. In addition, any area of collecting with as much history behind it as the American Indian is always made more interesting with a litte research. It gives you a much greater appreciation for what you collect. Try it . . . you'll like it!

Row 1: (1) $15.00-18.00   (2) $18.00-20.00   (3) $15.00-18.00

Row 2: (1) $10.00-12.00   (2) $35.00-40.00   (3) $10.00-12.00

Row 3: (1) $18.00-20.00   (2) $10.00-12.00   (3) $18.00-20.00

Row 4: (1) $12.00-15.00   (2) $10.00-12.00   (3) $12.00-15.00

Row 5: (1) $8.00-10.00   (2) $6.00-8.00   (3) $6.00-8.00   (4) $8.00-10.00

People: International Style

Dutch couples are shown on the first page, In imitation of Delft ware, the colors blue and white are often used on these shakers. The sets at the end of the first and last rows, however, are modern-day Delft and are marked "Holland."

The last set in the fourth row is another fine one from the Ceramic Art Studio in Wisconsin. The good detail and soft colors make this a very desirable pair--especially since the little boy looks so much like the one on the Dutch Boy Paint logo! Equally appealing, although not as high in quality, is the little kissing couple in the center of this row. He is holding a boat behind him and she is holding flowers--an altogether charming set.

The first two shelves on the next page picture some desirable Oriental shakers with their very detailed, brightly colored costumes. The last shaker set in Row Four has a "carved wood" look; they are, however, made of ceramic. The set of Eskimos on the bottom shelf, on the other hand, is the only one in this section made of porcelain. None of the sets pictured on this page are over three and one-half inches.

Also very popular are the bride and groom sets, forming the focal point of many other collections and so, on the last page, here come the brides. . . The bride in the third set on the top shelf is very detailed . . . she wears a REAL veil and gown! A trifle impractical for use as a salt shaker, wouldn't you say? The other brides are more suitably made (thank goodness).

The rest of the sets on this page are rather large, ranging in size from four and one-half to six inches high. Set two in the second row once held one of those "never-to-squeak-again" squeakers. The last set in this row is a nodder, another creation of the madman let loose in the design department.

The head of each shaker is attached by a spring . . . and spring it could--right into your food at any given moment. If anyone dared to use this set, the shaker was rather inconveniently contained in the body.

In the next row is a large Scottish couple dressed in the traditional fashion of their country. They are made of a heavy ceramic with a high glaze over rather muted colors. A very young Colonial couple (Thomas Jefferson and Betsy Ross?) are next; he displays the Bill of Rights and she the flag.

I'm sure a few of my friends out there can relate to the next set . . . Across the tummy of this rather disgruntled mother-to-be is written: "You and your one more for old times sake . . ." One more DANCE (the choice of the last couple on this shelf) may have been a whole lot safer!

The fourth row features two pair of Dutch children kissing; only the colors on these sets differ. The sets in the center are two-piece shakers. The person is the salt and the chair the pepper. These sets may have been made in a ceramics class or workshop since they do not appear to be commercially made and are unmarked.

The Oriental set on the bottom shelf was made by the Ceramic Art Studio of Wisconsin and demonstrates again the fine quality produced by this company. The last set on the page is a Mexican "kissing couple." I have never seen another set like it--which makes it pretty special (to me, at least).

Unless otherwise specified, all sets in this section are ceramic and were made in Japan. The majority of them are from the 1940-1950 era but a few of the sets were made as late as the 1970's.

Page 143

Row 1: (1) $10.00-12.00	(2) $6.00-8.00	(3) $10.00-12.00
Row 2: (1) $8.00-10.00	(2) $6.00-8.00	(3) $8.00-10.00
Row 3: (1) $8.00-10.00	(2) $8.00-10.00	(3) $6.00-8.00
Row 4: (1) $8.00-10.00	(2) $8.00-10.00	(3) $22.00-25.00
Row 5: (1) $8.00-10.00	(2) $10.00-12.00	(3) $10.00-12.00

Page 144

Row 1: All Sets $8.00-10.00			
Row 2: All Sets $8.00-10.00			
Row 3: All Sets $8.00-10.00			
Row 4: All Sets $8.00-10.00			
Row 5: (1) $10.00-12.00	(2) $8.00-10.00	(3) $8.00-10.00	(4) $10.00-12.00

Page 145

Row 1: (1) $10.00-12.00	(2) $6.00-8.00	(3) $12.00-15.00	(4) $10.00-12.00
Row 2: (1) $12.00-15.00	(2) $6.00-8.00	(3) $6.00-8.00	(4) $20.00-25.00
Row 3: (1) $12.00-15.00	(2) $10.00-12.00	(3) $10.00-12.00	(4) $12.00-15.00
Row 4: (1) $12.00-15.00	(2) $6.00-8.00	(3) $6.00-8.00	
Row 5: (1) $10.00-12.00	(2) $8.00-10.00	(3) $28.00-30.00	(4) $12.00-15.00

People: Presidents

This is a very small sampling of the presidential sets to be found. Although it would be a challenge, it is possible to collect a complete series of all the presidents to date--and all in salt and pepper form!

On the top shelf is pictured one of the best-loved presidents, John F. Kennedy, our 35th president. The center set pictured is the very popular one of Kennedy in his rocking chair. He was known to have spent a lot of time in his rocker because of his bad back, resulting from a war injury. In this particular set, the figure is the salt and the rocker the pepper. The shakers on either side are a set picturing Kennedy and his wife Jacqueline.

The second row features three different sets of George and Martha Washington. Considering that he was our first president, it comes as no surprise that these sets are also very popular. There are probably more souvenirs with the picture of George Washington on them than any other president we have ever had.

Finally, on the bottom row is a set picturing a former president who left the American people with very mixed feelings and some confusion--our 37th president, Richard Nixon and his wife Pat. For many reasons, he will always be one of our most unforgetable chief executives.

The last set on the page has the portrait of our 7th president, Andrew Jackson, on both shakers.

The only set marked is that of Kennedy in his rocker and it was made in Japan. The other shakers I believe were American-made, possibly as blanks with the decals added later by distributors throughout the country. I do know that there is an entire collection of shakers featuring the faces of all the presidents of the United States and that there are other figural-type sets to be found. Some of them are busts and some are full figures. In any event, if anyone out there has a complete series, I would enjoy seeing photographs of full sets of presidents--no matter what type of series. What a wonderful collection that would be to pass on to future generations.

* Note: Row 1-Set 2 $30.00-35.00 with *brown pants*.

Row 1: (1) $15.00-18.00 (Set)   * (2) $35.00-40.00   (3) $15.00-18.00 (Set)

Row 2: (1) $10.00-12.00   (2) $12.00-15.00   (3) $8.00-10.00

Row 3: (1) $8.00-10.00   (2) $6.00-8.00

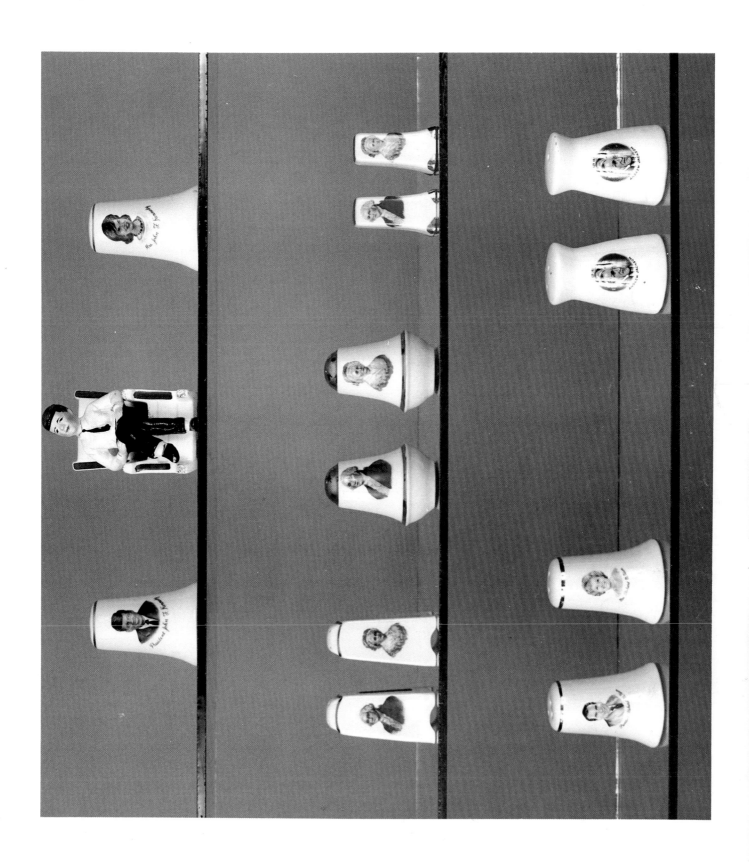

People: Santa Claus

Father Christmas, Saint Nicholas or Santa Claus--no matter what name we give him, he is still the same jolly, red-faced, bearded fellow in the red suit and loved by all of us. He is the recipient of more mail in December than the IRS in April and he is impersonated by more individuals than any other character known to man. Santa is a tradition, a legend, the hope of children everywhere and the wellspring of fond memories for most of us.

Because of all this and more, Santa is extremely popular with collectors. He is collected in postcards, ornaments, calendars and bells as well as salt and pepper shakers. There is an unlimited selection of Santa and Christmas shakers to be collected, and every year, there are new ones put on the market during the holiday season. Incidentally, as a general rule, the thinner the Santa, the earlier he is.

On this page is pictured a selection of "Mr. and Mrs." Santa sets, as well as the more traditional sets of Santa alone. Until this very moment, many of you may not have realized that one year Santa's sleigh broke down and he delivered Christmas gifts riding a PIG. Well, the third set in the third row features this historic moment . . . it was the year Santa brought home the bacon!

On the top row, the second set shows Santa with a gold-painted cap rather than the usual red one. The third set on this shelf is one of the oldest ones pictured and is very well detailed with its lacy decorations.

The first set in the second row shows Santa and Mrs. Santa waiting for Christmas letters from children. The next two sets are older ones and quite nice. You'll notice that Mrs. Santa--third set on the shelf--has lost some of her red paint. For some reason, red paint is very easily chipped and this flaking condition is quite common on shakers decorated with that color. The last set shown is made of plastic.

In the third row, Santa is winking and waving and riding a Pig . . . and trimming a tree without missing a twig. . . (I *was* going to write the entire book in poetry, but decided to spare you!)

On the bottom row, Santa bids us all farewell until next year. In the center, he and the Missus are resting after a busy season and the last set wishes all of us a "Merry Christmas."

These are just a few of the hundreds of sets to be found. Santa sets are really fun to collect--especially if you can find Santa on a pig! Unless otherwise noted, all the sets on this page are pre-1960, ceramic and made in Japan.

Row 1: (1) $8.00-10.00	(2) $10.00-12.00	(3) $12.00-15.00	(4) $8.00-10.00
Row 2: (1) $8.00-10.00	(2) $12.00-15.00	(3) $12.00-15.00	(4) $6.00-8.00
Row 3: (1) $5.00-7.00	(2) $12.00-15.00	(3) $15.00-18.00	(4) $8.00-10.00
Row 4: (1) $15.00-18.00	(2) $15.00-18.00	(3) $12.00-15.00	

People: Santa Claus and Christmas

When was the last time you built a snowman? As children, we used to make huge snowmen each winter that looked like the shaker sets shown at the top of the page. Since all the shakers on this page represent winter and/or Christmas in some way, they can easily be included with a Santa collection. The snowmen all look great in their top hats and the snowwoman looks so cute in her little bonnet. The last set on the shelf makes it very easy to determine which shaker is salt and which is pepper--a convenience much appreciated by those who may have imbibed too much "holiday cheer."

The second row features angels with gifts and three sets of children. The second set is very sweet with little girls holding delicate snowflakes. The children in the last set are riding small sleighs and look like they are truly enjoying themselves.

Santa's reindeer in the next row are all bedecked in bells. The rather haughty Santa and his snooty reindeer have magnets on the side of the shakers so they don't lose each other.

On the bottom of the page are gifts, elegantly wrapped and tagged "Salt and Pepper." The candy-cane people next to them leave a lot to be desired . . they look like they were made from leftover pieces of ceramic clay! The candle set, however, would look beautiful on a Christmas dinner table. It has such charm with the deep green leaves, red bow and golden flame accents.

The last set pictured is rather large. They were the original shoes worn by Santa's first Elf . . . and I PROMISE that this is the last of my "Christmas humor." Again, all the sets are pre-1960 and made in Japan.

Row 1: (1) $10.00-12.00   (2) $8.00-10.00   (3) $8.00-10.00   (4) $10.00-12.00

Row 2: (1) $10.00-12.00   (2) $8.00-10.00   (3) $8.00-10.00   (4) $8.00-10.00

Row 3: All Sets $8.00-10.00

Row 4: All Sets $8.00-10.00

Vegetable and Fruit People

Of all the types of shakers in my collection, these little vegetable and fruit people, especially the ones trimmed with lace, are among my top favorites. They are all so cute--the little rabbits looking out of the carrots and the elves under the asparagus, the corn people and so on.

Most of the sets are two of the same vegetable or fruit, but there are a few mixed sets on the bottom row. I have a children's book, *Aunt Este's Stories of the Vegetable and Fruit Children*, written by Edna Groff Deihl and published in 1923. The stories tell about the "Fruit Folk" like the Banana Family and their "bunch" of children. Hans Christian Cauliflower has a few adventures of his own while the romance of Billy Bartlett and Sickle Pear furnishes material for another tale. Goldie Peach and Honey Plum together with the Pea Children all add up to an absolutely delightful book well worth looking for. Although I had the sets of salt and peppers long before I found the book, "Aunt Este's Stories" added a special dimension to the collection.

Most of the sets with lace trim are made of porcelain; the detail and coloring on these are superb. The other sets are ceramic and most all of them are hand-painted. All were manufactured in Japan. Although dating them is difficult, I would place them around the 1930's and early 1940's. Maybe they were inspired by the book!

I see very few of these sets around this area anymore. They may be easier to find elsewhere but, since they are absolutely adorable to collect, they are worth searching for.

Row 1: All Sets $15.00-20.00

Row 2: (1) $8.00-10.00   (2) $8.00-10.00   (3) $12.00-15.00   (4) $12.00-15.00   (5) $8.00-10.00

Row 3: (1) $12.00-15.00   (2) $6.00-8.00   (3) $12.00-15.00   (4) $12.00-15.00   (5) $12.00-15.00

Row 4: All Sets $12.00-15.00

Row 5: (1) $12.00-15.00   (2) $8.00-10.00   (3) $12.00-15.00   (4) $12.00-15.00

Vegetable and Fruit People (continued)

The sets pictured here are of a later vintage than those on the preceding page. Tennis and baseball players and even artists are in the group. (I guess you could call them the action bunch . . .) I included the fork, spoon and teapot people. If you plan to eat the vegetable people, after all, it should at least be with fork or spoon people!

The whimsy of these sets is charming and they seem to trigger my imagination. Think of little voices yelling as you bite into an apple or an ear of corn! Or picture all the vegetables holding a dance in your refrigerator. Just keep in mind Fruit and Vegetables are People, too.

Most of the sets on this page are from the 1940's and 1950's and made of ceramic; most are hand-painted and again all are made in Japan.

Row 1: (1) $22.00-25.00   (2) $12.00-15.00   (3) $18.00-20.00   (4) $22.00-25.00

Row 2: All Sets $20.00-23.00

Row 3: (1) $12.00-15.00   (2) $8.00-10.00   (3) $8.00-10.00   (4) $12.00-15.00

Row 4: All Sets $6.00-8.00

People: Miscellaneous

"People ARE funny" as Art Linkletter used to say, and the people who populate the world of salt-and-pepper shakers are no exceptions. The next two pages present a variety of "people shakers" almost too varied to be believed and certainly too numerous to describe individually. Of all the figural shakers on the market, representations of people comprise more than half. As you can see from the many sets pictured throughout the book, collectors can choose many different areas of specialization using just the variations of the human form.

On the first page, the top row features larger sets. "Old Salty and Cap'n Pepper" are about six inches tall. They are made of a chalk-like ceramic and handpainted with a matte finish. The baseball players in the first and last rows have great comic detail. These sets are painted under the glaze on a heavy ceramic body. The third set in the second row looks like characters from the old Toonerville cartoon series . . . but I don't know who they would be. Even hippies from the 1960's are represented in the last row.

Cowboys, castle guards, pixies, wrestlers, mounties or nuns . . . the choice is *yours*.

The second page pictures toby-type salt-and-pepper sets and bust sets. The tobies, which are all the sets pictured in the first two rows, are the most popular with collectors. The sets on the first shelf are less than one and one half inches high, very detailed and beautifully painted (as are the larger toby-types on the second shelf.) On the last three rows are busts. The detail on the set of two old men in the center is fantastic, but all of the faces are interesting. The busts of two rather dainty women at the far right of the bottom row, however, are very delicate and pleasant compared to the rather exaggerated qualities of the other sets.

A few of the sets pictured are not marked, but I believe they were all made in Japan between 1940 and present.

Page 157

Row 1: (1) $8.00-10.00	(2) $8.00-10.00	(3) $15.00-18.00	
Row 2: (1) $6.00-8.00	(2) $5.00-7.00	(3) $20.00-25.00	(4) $15.00-18.00
Row 3: (1) $7.00-9.00	(2) $18.00-20.00	(3) $18.00-20.00	(4) $15.00-18.00
Row 4: All Sets $7.00-9.00			
Row 5: All Sets $15.00-18.00			

Page 158

Row 1: All Sets $8.00-10.00			
Row 2: All Sets $8.00-10.00			
Row 3: (1) $6.00-8.00	(2) $8.00-10.00	(3) $6.00-8.00	
Row 4: All Sets $6.00-8.00			
Row 5: (1) $6.00-8.00	(2) $6.00-8.00	(3) $6.00-8.00	(4) $10.00-12.00

157

Bibliography

------*Avon*, Western World Publisher. San Francisco, California.

Florence, Gene. *The Collectors' Encyclopedia of Occupied Japan*, Series 1 and 2. Collector Books, Paducah, Kentucky.

Kay, Robert E. *Miniature Beer Bottles and Go-Withs*. 216 Batavia, Illinois 60510. (order directly from author).

Klamkin, Marian. *Made in Occupied Japan*. Crown Publishers, New York. (1976)

Lechner, Mildred and Ralph. *The World of Salt Shakers*. Collector Books, Paducah, Kentucky.

Peterson, Arthur G. *Glass Salt Shakers, 1000 Patterns*.

Reddock, Richard and Barbara. *Planters Peanuts Advertising and Collectibles*. 914 Isle Court, Bellmore, New York 11710.

Robinson, Joleen and Sellers, Kay F. *Advertising Dolls*. Collector Books, Paducah, Kentucky. (1980)

Simon, Dolores H. *Shawnee Pottery*. Collector Books, Paducah, Kentucky.

Westfall, Ermagene. *Cookie Jars*. Collector Books, Paducah, Kentucky.

Newsletter

"Novelty Salt and Pepper Club" c/o Irene Thornburg, 581 Joy Rd., Battle Creek, MI 49017 - (Over 800 members.)

Schroeder's Antiques Price Guide

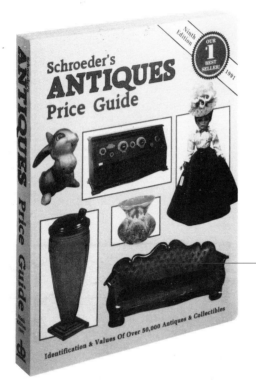

Schroeder's Antiques Price Guide has become THE household name in the antiques & collectibles industry. Our team of editors work year around with more than 200 contributors to bring you our #1 best-selling book on antiques & collectibles.

With more than 50,000 items identified & priced, Schroeder's is a must for the collector & dealer alike. If it merits the interest of today's collector, you'll find it in Schroeder's. Each subject is represented with histories and background information. In addition, hundreds of sharp original photos are used each year to illustrate not only the rare and unusual, but the everyday "fun-type" collectibles as well -- not postage stamp pictures, but large close-up shots that show important details clearly.

Our editors compile a new book each year. Never do we merely change prices. Accuracy is our primary aim. Prices are gathered over the entire year previous to publication, from ads and personal contacts. Then each category is thoroughly checked to spot inconsistencies, listings that may not be entirely reflective of actual market dealings, and lines too vague to be of merit. Only the best of the lot remains for publication. You'll find Schroeder's Antiques Price Guide the one to buy for factual information and quality.

No dealer, collector or investor can afford not to own this book. It is available from your favorite bookseller or antiques dealer at the low price of $12.95. If you are unable to find this price guide in your area, it's available from Collector Books, P.O. Box 3009, Paducah, KY 42001 at $12.95 plus $2.00 for postage and handling.

8½ x 11", 608 Pages　　　　　　　　　　　　　　　　　　　　　　　**$12.95**

COLLECTOR BOOKS

A Division of Schroeder Publishing Co., Inc.